20-Minute Dinners

20-Minute Dinners

Mary B. Johnson

STERLING
INNOVATION
A Division of Sterling Publishing Co., Inc.
New York

Library of Congress Cataloging-in-Publication Data Available

2 4 6 8 10 9 7 5 3 1

Published in 2007 by Sterling Publishing Co., Inc.
387 Park Avenue South, New York, NY 10016
Originally published as *Quick Cooks' Kitchen: 20-Minute Meals*

© 2004 by Sterling Publishing Co., Inc.
Photographs © 2004 by Theresa Raffetto

Distributed in Canada by Sterling Publishing
c/o Canadian Manda Group, 165 Dufferin Street
Toronto, Ontario, Canada M6K 3H6
Distributed in the United Kingdom by GMC Distribution Services
Castle Place, 166 High Street, Lewes, East Sussex, England BN7 1XU
Distributed in Australia by Capricorn Link (Australia) Pty. Ltd.
P.O. Box 704, Windsor, NSW 2756, Australia

Design by Liz Trovato
Edited by Pamela Horn

Photographs by Theresa Raffetto
Food Stylist: Victoria Granof
Prop Stylist: Sharon Ryan

Printed in China
All rights reserved

Sterling ISBN-13: 978-1-4027-4348-1
ISBN-10: 1-4027-4348-3

For information about custom editions, special sales, premium and
corporate purchases, please contact Sterling Special Sales
Department at 800-805-5489 or specialsales@sterlingpub.com.

Introduction

With so many options for a quick meal—quality frozen, prepped, and ready-to-heat foods; take-out and delivery; and microwavable everything—there seems to be little reason to cook! Now *20-Minute Dinners* provides you with 76 themed menus—over 250 recipes—that are full of home-cooked goodness to satisfy the busy cook in us all.

"Home cooking" is anything you want it to be: Just because it has to be done on the run doesn't mean you can't have all the comforting aromas and flavors of a home-cooked meal. All it really takes is organization and focus. The 20-minute goal is in real time, so once you start Step 1, you can relax and anticipate an on-time arrival at the table!

From a light Spring meal to a tasty menu for bridesmaids; a New Year's Eve late supper to mid-week dinners, a cocktail party, and an antipasto spread, you'll see recipes for a wide variety of meals and cuisines. Some have international origins; some are decidedly domestic. There truly is something for everyone in these pages!

Cooks' Tips

Efficiency shouldn't equate with frenzy: we have a game plan or strategy for each menu that will help to keep you calm. If you are wondering how you can put a meal on your table with relative ease—here are some tips:

• Read the recipe from start to finish before beginning your prep. Make sure you understand the directions and reread anything that seems unclear to you.

• Start by getting all of your ingredients within reach and do all of your prep work before beginning to cook. That way, you can cruise through the instructions and whip up a great meal in no time.

• It helps to have a few trusty staples you can rely on. Some of the pantry basics used in this book are sold in specialty food stores, so recipes are given for them in case you can't find them or you've used up your supply. Each of these pantry staples is a tasty timesaver that greatly cuts down on your steps in the kitchen.

• With a multitasking mindset, you'll discover more packaged products that cut down on prep time, cooking, and cleanup.

Basic Tools

You can create any of the recipes in this book with just a few basic kitchen tools. You don't need all of the items—just some staples to put that 20-minute goal within your reach:

Cutting board: At least one board in either wood or plastic is a must-have. Whichever you choose, be sure to get one large enough for unhindered chopping, yet small enough for easy washing. For food safety, remember to use separate boards (or separate sides of one board) for cutting produce and raw meats and to wash the boards thoroughly between uses.

Chef's knife: Select a top-quality knife and keep it sharp for optimum performance. This knife comes in 6-, 8-, 10-, and 12-inch lengths. The 8-inch one gets our vote for versatility. It lets you cut meats, chop vegetables, and mince garlic and herbs in no time flat.

Paring knife: A paring knife usually comes with a 3- or 4-inch blade and makes short work of trimming mushrooms, peeling fruits, and other similar tasks.

Vegetable peeler: This tool is ideal for peeling thin-skinned root vegetables such as carrots, potatoes, parsnips, and even young butternut squash. Find a peeler with a swivel blade and a comfortable handle.

Measuring cups and spoons: Get a nested set of dry measuring cups for measuring rice, pasta, beans, and frozen peas and corn. Use a liquid measure for broth, tomatoes, and other liquid ingredients. The same set of nested spoons can be used for dry and wet items.

Wooden spoons: Wooden spoons are good for most mixing and stirring tasks. They don't scratch pots, pans, or dishes, and their shallow bowls are perfectly suited for stirring. Their handles stay cool, and don't melt if you accidentally leave them touching a hot pot.

Saucepans and pots: The saucepan is the smaller of the two and has one handle; the pot is larger and has two handles. The pot, however, will give you more room for stirring and gentle simmering. Make sure you get a snug-fitting lid for whatever you have. The pot itself should be heavy and a non-stick interior is not necessary.

Immersion blender: This handy gadget allows you to purée ingredients directly in the pot. If you don't have one, a blender, food processor, food mill, or potato masher will work.

And last but not least, make sure you have a trusty can opener!

Note: The recipe listings throughout the actual menus may contain italicized items. All that means is that we have included foods to fill out the menu but have not provided a recipe. Purchasing these items will get you to your 20-minute goal without a doubt.

Menus

Easy Antipasto Dinner Party

Antipasto Buffet Platter
Black Bean and Butternut Squash
    Bruschetta
Broiled Fig and Prosciutto Bruschetta
Grilled Summer Squash Bruschetta
Sliced Raw Mushrooms with Lemon
Marinated Chickpeas

page 158

Sunday Dinner for Company

Peach Bellinis
Grilled Mustard-Dill Salmon
Linguine with Asparagus and
    Lemon Cream Sauce
Candied Apricots and Sweet Cheese Bites

page 162

Virtual-Island-Vacation Supper

Quesadilla Grande
Poached Salmon Medallions with
    Guacamole
Marinated Three-Bean Salad
Passionate Pineapple Parfaits

page 164

Southern Sunday Dinner

Tupelo Honey-Roasted Pork Tenderloin
Sweet Potatoes in Star Anise Broth
Quick Coconut Cake

page 166

"Who Really Needs a Villa?" Feast

Tuscan Squab
Penne with Pesto, Porcini, and Peas
Cauliflower with Anchovy-Caper Sauce
Favorite Gelato

page 169

Steak Lover's Delight

Beef with Peppercorn Sauce
Kasha with Bow-Tie Pasta
Mizuna with Roasted Onions

page 172

Family-Style Flavors

Skillet-Barbecued Chicken with Peppers
Pork and Beans
Mom's Grilled Peaches
Cookie and Ice-Cream Sandwiches

page 174

Fusion Italian Dinner

Steamed Chicken Rolls
Pappardelle alla Vodka
Broccoli with Lemon-Garlic Crumbs

page 176

Fun Fusion Flavors

• Smoked-Mozzarella and Tomato Salad • Pan-Seared Halibut with Oregano-Tahini Glaze • Garlic Green Beans

MAKES 4 SERVINGS

Classic and innovative care with ingredients is an art as well as a science. This combination is really instinctive. What's not to like?

GAME PLAN

1. Assemble salad.
2. Prepare and cook fish.
3. Cook beans and toss with seasonings.

Smoked-Mozzarella and Tomato Salad

Use heirloom tomatoes if they are in season. Slice them instead of chopping in order to showcase their beauty.

2 tablespoons pine nuts

1/4 cup extra-virgin olive oil

2 tablespoons red-wine vinegar

sea salt and freshly ground black pepper to taste

4 ripe tomatoes, coarsely chopped

1 pound smoked mozzarella, sliced into 1/4-inch-thick rounds

8 fresh basil leaves, torn

• Toast pine nuts in small nonstick skillet over medium heat until golden, about 4 minutes (watch carefully so they don't scorch). Pour into a cup.

• Mix oil, vinegar, salt, and pepper in a large bowl; add tomatoes and toss to coat.

• Arrange cheese on plates; top with tomatoes. Sprinkle with basil and pine nuts.

Pan-Seared Halibut with Oregano-Tahini Glaze

1/4 cup tahini (sesame seed paste)

3 tablespoons fresh lemon juice

1 tablespoon dried oregano leaves

1 teaspoon seasoned salt

4 (1-inch-thick) halibut steaks (2 pounds)

2 tablespoons unsalted butter

2 tablespoons olive oil

• Mix tahini, lemon juice, oregano, and salt in small bowl; brush mixture on both sides of steaks.

• Melt butter in oil in a large nonstick skillet over medium-high heat. Add steaks, cover, and cook over medium heat until browned, 3 to 4 minutes. Turn steaks and cook, covered, until done, 3 to 4 minutes.

Garlic Green Beans

2 (10-ounce) packages French-cut green beans

1 tablespoon extra-virgin olive oil

3/4 teaspoon garlic salt

1/2 teaspoon freshly ground black pepper

• Cook beans as package label directs; drain and toss with oil, salt, and pepper.

Meat and Potatoes Skillet Dinner

• Skillet Shepherd's Pie • Carrot and Dried Fruit Salad • Ginger Fool with Pappadams

MAKES 4 SERVINGS

Built around a one-pot stovetop main course, this meal draws in a quickly assembled supporting cast with many surprising flavor combinations and textures. Pappadams are a crisp wafer used in Indian cuisine, usually made with chickpea flour to accompany curries. Here is a twist for a surprising dessert.

GAME PLAN
1. Preheat broiler; brown lamb. Soak dried fruit.
2. Make fool; refrigerate. Finish shepherd's pie and broil.
3. Toss salad. Fry or microwave pappadams.

Skillet Shepherd's Pie

1 tablespoon vegetable oil
1 pound lamb sausages, removed from casings
1 bunch green onions, trimmed, chopped
1 1/4 cups chicken stock or water
1 (1 1/4-pound) pouch refrigerated mashed potatoes
  or 3 cups prepared instant or leftover mashed
  potatoes
1 cup fresh or frozen peas
1/4 cup bottled mint sauce or mint jelly with
  mint leaves
2 tablespoons grated Parmigiano-Reggiano cheese

• Preheat broiler. Heat oil over medium-high heat in a medium skillet with an ovenproof handle. Add sausage and sauté, crumbling into small chunks, until browned, about 5 minutes.

• Drain off fat; add onions and sauté 1 minute. Add chicken stock, 1 cup potatoes, and peas; heat to boiling, adding mint sauce. Stir until thickened.

• Spoon remaining potatoes on top; spread with a fork, making swirls with tines. Sprinkle with cheese. Broil 6 inches from heat source until browned. Serve from skillet.

Carrot and Dried Fruit Salad

*1 cup raspberry or citrus vinaigrette (store-bought, or
see recipes page 216)*
*1 cup mixed currants, golden and dark raisins, and
other chopped dried fruits (dates, apricots,
cranberries, etc.)*
*1 (10-ounce) bag shredded carrots or 2 cups
julienned carrots*

• Heat vinaigrette in bowl in microwave or saucepan;
add fruit. Stir and let stand until softened, about 5
minutes. Drain, reserving liquid. Add carrots to fruit
and toss. Add enough reserved vinaigrette to coat.

Ginger Fool with Pappadams

*¹/2 cup ginger marmalade or ¹/2 cup chopped
crystallized ginger*
1 (8-ounce) container vanilla pudding
1 cup vanilla yogurt
oil for shallow frying
4 pappadams, plain or with black pepper

• Mix marmalade with pudding in a medium shallow
glass bowl. Stir yogurt with a fork until creamy; pour
in a swirl pattern over the pudding mixture and draw
a knife into the swirl lines to mix. Refrigerate.

• Heat oil in small saucepan and fry pappadams as
package label directs. Drain and cool. Serve with
Ginger Fool.

BUY TIME

If you can find them, some brands of pappadams can
be microwaved as well as fried. They are a little more
expensive than the classic frying-only kind, but they save
valuable time.

20 Minutes 'til Cocktails

• Cold Ginger-Crabmeat Dip • *Store-Bought Chicken Wings*
• Quick Tonnato Sauce • Hearts of Palm and Tomato Platter
• Blue Cheese Wedge • *Seedless Grapes* • *Crackers* • *Store-Bought Crudités*

MAKES 4 SERVINGS

You may hit the door and say to yourself, "Whose idea was this anyway!" But relax. You'll have time to put everything out and still freshen up. Just pick up chicken wings from the grocery store, deli, or Chinese/pizza joint take-out and buy pre-cut raw vegetables from the grocery store produce department for an easy crudité platter.

GAME PLAN
1. Warm wings in oven. Make dip.
2. Make Tonnato Sauce.
3. Assemble vegetable platter.

Cold Ginger-Crabmeat Dip

1 pound jumbo lump crabmeat, gently picked over for bits of shells
1 (8-ounce) can water chestnuts, drained, rinsed, chopped
2 tablespoons garlic teriyaki sauce or ginger-flavored low-sodium soy sauce
1 cup sour cream
1 tablespoon grated peeled fresh gingerroot
celery sticks for dipping

• Gently mix ingredients except celery in a medium bowl. Cover and chill if schedule permits. Serve with celery sticks.

Makes 4 to 6 servings.

Quick Tonnato Sauce

1 cup bottled tartar sauce

1 can (around 6 ounces) tuna (water- or oil-packed),
*   drained*

1 anchovy

1 tablespoon fresh lemon juice or more to taste

2 tablespoons olive oil or more if needed

● Purée tartar sauce, tuna, anchovy, and 1 table-spoon lemon juice in food processor; with machine running, pour in oil. Taste; add more lemon juice if needed.

Makes 4 servings.

Hearts of Palm and Tomato Platter

1 (10-ounce) bag romaine lettuce pieces

1 (14-ounce) can hearts of palm, drained

1/2 pint red grape or pear tomatoes

1/2 pint yellow grape or pear tomatoes

1/4 cup mixed imported olives

red-wine vinaigrette (store-bought, or see recipe
*   page 216)*

● Arrange lettuce on a platter. Top with hearts of palm, tomatoes, and olives. Drizzle with vinaigrette and toss and serve as a salad; or pour vinaigrette in a bowl and serve as an antipasto with wooden picks for dipping hearts of palm and tomatoes.

COOK'S TIP

Tonnato Sauce is traditionally used as an accompaniment to a veal roast or cutlet. Here it makes a tasty transformation into a quick dip for crudités.

Après-Ski/Snowboard Feeding Frenzy

• Melting Mustard Cheese • Texas "Caviar" Dip • Chocolate–Peanut Butter Fondue • Hot Spiced Lemonade

MAKES 6 SERVINGS

After burning all those calories on the slope, it's time to eat! Replenish with some delicious and easy food. Here are some quickly assembled, nutritious (yet indulgent) hunger-busters.

GAME PLAN

1. Heat lemonade. Make cheese mixture.
2. Mix caviar. Make fondue.
3. Assemble dippers; heat franks; cut fruit.

Melting Mustard Cheese

Not quite a fondue, this is a tasty warm dip.

1 (8-ounce) package chive-, bacon-, or sun-dried tomato-flavored or plain cream cheese, softened

1/4 cup ginger ale or beer

1 teaspoon hot English or Chinese mustard

2 cups (8 ounces) shredded cheddar cheese

2-inch chunks of celery for dipping

little frankfurters (heated) for dipping

• Place cream cheese, ginger ale, and mustard in medium microwave-safe bowl. Cover with microwave-safe plastic wrap; microwave on high power until cream cheese is softened, 2 minutes. Stir until smooth. Stir in cheddar cheese until blended. Microwave until cheese is melted, stirring every minute, for 2 to 3 minutes. Serve in a shallow bowl or dish on a warming tray, with celery and frankfurters for dipping.

Makes about 3 cups.

Texas "Caviar" Dip

The protein combo of beans and corn from the hominy and the tortilla chips makes this an incredibly nutritious snack.

1 (14-ounce) can black-eyed peas, drained, rinsed
1 (15¹/2-ounce) can white hominy, drained, rinsed
1 green bell pepper, seeded, chopped
1 cup salsa fresca (store-bought, or see recipe
   page 215)
1 cup bottled hot picante sauce
tortilla chips for dipping

● Mix black-eyed peas, hominy, pepper, salsa, and picante sauce in medium bowl. Serve with tortilla chips.

Makes about 6 cups.

Chocolate–Peanut Butter Fondue

4 ounces semisweet chocolate, chopped
1 (14-ounce) can sweetened condensed milk
¹/2 cup milk
¹/4 cup peanut butter
apple slices, grapes, strawberries, tangerine or
   clementine segments, pretzels, etc., for dipping

● Combine chocolate, condensed milk, milk, and peanut butter in microwave-safe bowl; cover with microwave-safe plastic wrap. Heat on high power 3 minutes; stir. Cover and heat, stirring every 1 minute, until chocolate melts and mixture is smooth, about 3 minutes. Serve in a fondue pot or place bowl on a warming tray. Serve with dippers (use skewers for dipping grapes).

Hot Spiced Lemonade

1 quart lemonade
2 cups water
2 (3-inch) cinnamon sticks
2 (.72-ounce) packets apple-cider mix or ¹/3 cup
   spiced-tea mix

● Heat lemonade, water, and cinnamon sticks in 2-quart saucepan until almost boiling; add cider mix. Stir until dissolved. Pour into an insulated pitcher.

Makes 6 to 8 servings.

Dinner with Elbows on the Table

• Mussels Steamed in Salsa Broth • Burgers Oozing Cheese • Bean and Orange Salad

MAKES 4 SERVINGS

Eat mussels with your fingers, dunking your bread in the savory broth, then digging into gooey cheeseburgers. This is a meal made for the shoeless, the plaid flannel–shirted; in short, it's for family and good friends.

GAME PLAN
1. Soak onions. Stuff burgers.
2. Combine mussels with other ingredients in pan. Make salad.
3. Cook burgers. Steam mussels.

Mussels Steamed in Salsa Broth

2 pounds mussels, scrubbed, de-bearded
2 cups mild salsa (as low-salt as possible)
1 cup vermouth (red or white, sweet or dry)
1 cup water
1 bunch green onions, trimmed, chopped
flour tortillas or crusty bread for dunking

• Combine mussels, salsa, vermouth, and water in large deep skillet and heat to boiling. Cover and steam 1 minute. Stir to make sure all mussels are positioned so they can open. Steam until mussels open, about 4 minutes.

• Discard unopened mussels. Stir in green onions; spoon into bowls, and use tortillas or bread to scoop up the mussels and sop up the broth.

Burgers Oozing Cheese

Serve on buns, open-faced on English muffin halves, or on a bed of shredded lettuce.

1 (5-ounce) package imported garlic-and-herb
   cheese spread
1¹/2 pounds ground sirloin
kosher salt and freshly ground pepper to taste

● Cut cheese into 4 rounds. Shape sirloin into 8 thin patties. Place a cheese round on 4 patties; top with another patty. Press edges to seal cheese inside; sprinkle salt and pepper on both sides of burgers.

● Heat cast-iron grill pan or skillet over high heat. Cook burgers 2 minutes; turn 60° so grill marks will be dramatic. Cook 2 more minutes. Turn burgers and repeat for medium-rare. Cover loosely and let stand 5 minutes.

Bean and Orange Salad

1 small red onion, thinly sliced into rings
1 (15-ounce) can black beans, small red beans, or
   kidney beans, drained, rinsed
1 (11-ounce) can mandarin orange sections, drained
¹/4 cup fresh cilantro leaves
¹/3 cup fresh lime juice
salt and freshly ground pepper to taste

● Soak onion in ice water 10 minutes. Drain and pat dry with paper towel. Place in medium bowl and add remaining ingredients; toss to mix.

Quietly Dazzling Supper

• Crusty Fried Cheese Wedges • Sun-Dried Tomato Sauce • Fried Liver with Pancetta and Balsamic Glaze • Pear and Frisée Salad

MAKES 4 SERVINGS

Once again it's a case of simple food done well. It's not easy to fry cheese and liver under time constraints because there is an inclination to turn up the heat too much. So relax, and make "less is more" your mantra.

GAME PLAN

1. Coat cheese. Make sauce. Heat oil for cheese.
2. Cook pancetta; prepare salad.
3. Fry liver; keep warm. Fry cheese.

Crusty Fried Cheese Wedges

3/4 cup rice flour or all-purpose flour

1 egg

2 tablespoons water

3/4 cups fine plain dried white bread crumbs

1 teaspoon golden mustard seeds

1/2 teaspoon freshly ground coriander (optional)

1/4 teaspoon garlic salt

8 ounces firm cheese (but not a hard grating cheese) such as Comté, caciovallo, kasseri, Edam, Cheshire, or Monterey Jack, cut into 4 (1/2-inch-thick) wedges

vegetable oil for frying

Sun-Dried Tomato Sauce (recipe follows; optional)

• Place flour on a plate. Beat egg with water in a shallow bowl. Mix bread crumbs, mustard seeds, coriander, and salt on another plate.

• Coat cheese wedges with flour; shake off excess. Coat with egg; drain off excess. Coat completely with crumbs.

• Heat 2 inches oil until hot but not smoking in deep large skillet over medium-high heat. Using long-handled tongs, place wedges into oil (do not crowd) and fry until golden, turning once, about 2 minutes in all. Drain on paper towels. Serve with sauce.

Sun-Dried Tomato Sauce

1/4 cup marinated sun-dried tomatoes
1/4 cup pine nuts
1/4 cup fresh parsley leaves
1/4 teaspoon garlic powder or to taste
dash cayenne or crushed red-pepper flakes or to taste
3/4 to 1 cup tomato juice

• Purée tomatoes, nuts, parsley, garlic powder, and cayenne in food processor. With motor running, pour in 3/4 cup tomato juice. Heat in saucepan or microwave until hot; adjust thickness with additional tomato juice as needed.

Fried Liver with Pancetta and Balsamic Glaze

Not a liver lover? Use 1/2-inch-thick boneless steaks or chops; or veal, chicken, or turkey cutlets.

1/2 (10-ounce) jar marinated grilled cipollini
*   onions, marinating liquid reserved, onions*
*   quartered*
2 (1/4-inch-thick) slices pancetta, cut into 1-inch
*   slivers*
4 (6- to 8-ounce) slices beef or calves liver, 1/2 inch
*   thick*
salt and freshly ground black pepper to taste
1/2 cup mixed chopped red, yellow, and green bell
*   peppers*
1/2 cup balsamic vinegar

• Heat 2 tablespoons marinating liquid from onions in shallow heavy skillet over medium-high heat. Add pancetta and sauté until crisp, about 5 minutes. Remove with slotted spoon to a plate; keep warm.

• Sprinkle livers with salt and black pepper. Sauté liver in drippings until firm and golden brown on underside, about 3 minutes; turn over and sauté 3 minutes more. Remove to warm serving platter; cover loosely with foil.

• Add onions, peppers, vinegar, and black pepper to drippings in pan; sauté until vegetables are glazed. Pour over liver; sprinkle with pancetta.

Pear and Frisée Salad

1 bunch frisée, leaves torn
1/3 cup bottled Dijon vinaigrette
1 (8-ounce) can sliced pears in natural juices,
*   drained*

• Toss frisée with dressing in salad bowl to coat. Place on 4 plates. Top with pear slices.

GOT TIME?

Use 2 fresh pears, stems intact, peeled, halved, and cored instead of canned pears. Slice each pear lengthwise into 6 or 8 slices, keeping slices intact at stem end, and fan out each over the frisée.

Molto Presto Pasta Supper

• Fresh Ravioli with Hazelnut Sauce • Baby Spinach Salad • Frozen Lemon Tarts

MAKES 4 SERVINGS

Fresh ravioli is everywhere—thank goodness! It's an instant upscale meal that needs only a couple of tasty sidekicks. Spinach and lemon elements answer the call.

GAME PLAN

1. Heat water for ravioli. Make tarts.
2. Cook ravioli.
3. Make salad and hazelnut sauce.

Fresh Ravioli with Hazelnut Sauce

salt
1 pound fresh ravioli (filled as desired)
4 tablespoons unsalted butter
1/2 cup coarsely chopped hazelnuts
1/2 teaspoon freshly ground pepper
wedge of Parmigiano-Reggiano cheese

• Heat 2 quarts salted water in a deep skillet until boiling. Add ravioli and cook until al dente. Drain. Keep ravioli warm.

• In same skillet, melt butter and sauté nuts and pepper until nuts are browned and fragrant. Add ravioli and stir gently until coated. Slide into warmed serving bowl and shave cheese on top using a vegetable peeler or grater.

Baby Spinach Salad

4 cups washed baby spinach

2 tablespoons balsamic vinaigrette (store-bought, or see recipe page 215)

• Toss spinach with dressing in salad bowl until coated. Serve immediately.

Frozen Lemon Tarts

1 cup crushed shortbread cookies

2 tablespoons unsalted butter, melted

1/4 teaspoon cinnamon

1 1/4 cups lemon curd (store-bought, or see recipe page 218)

• Line 4 muffin tins or shallow custard cups with paper muffin cups. Mix cookie crumbs with butter and cinnamon in a bowl until blended.

• Pack one-fourth of mixture into each prepared cup using the bottom of a glass. Spoon curd into each and freeze until firm, at least 15 minutes. Lift up paper liners and place tarts onto plates to serve.

Bon Voyage Send Off Dinner

• Thai Roasted Chicken Salad • Spicy Peanut Noodles • Balsamic-Splashed Clementines

MAKES 4 SERVINGS

This celebratory meal can be used to wish friends luck on their new endeavors. The flavors are so good, they may never leave!

GAME PLAN

1. Heat water for noodles and soak. Cut and sprinkle clementines.
2. Cut up vegetables for salad and noodles.
3. Make salad and noodle dressings; add and toss.

Thai Roasted Chicken Salad

2 1/2-pound roasted chicken, skinned, boned, cut into
   3/4-inch pieces
1 English cucumber, halved lengthwise, seeded with
   a spoon, thinly sliced crosswise
3 green onions, trimmed, thinly sliced diagonally
1 small red bell pepper, seeded, julienned

DRESSING

1/4 cup Thai or Vietnamese fish sauce
   (nam pla or nuoc mam)
2 tablespoons brown sugar
2 tablespoons tamarind paste or lime juice
1 teaspoon ground coriander
1 teaspoon hot chili oil or to taste

GARNISH

1/4 cup chopped roasted peanuts
2 tablespoons shredded Thai or Italian basil leaves
   (do not shred in advance)

• Combine chicken and vegetables in large bowl.

• Combine fish sauce, brown sugar, tamarind paste, and coriander in blender or food processor and blend until smooth. Sample and add chili oil to taste. Pour over chicken mixture; toss to mix. Just before serving, sprinkle with peanuts and basil.

Spicy Peanut Noodles

1 (8-ounce) package curly Chinese noodles

1 envelope or cube chicken bouillon

1 cup boiling water

2 green onions, trimmed, cut into 2-inch pieces

2 large garlic cloves, peeled

1/2 cup natural smooth peanut butter, stirred

1/4 cup fresh lemon juice

1/4 cup low-sodium soy sauce

2 tablespoons dark sesame oil

1/2 teaspoon crushed red pepper flakes or Indonesian
    sambal oelek (Indonesian chili sauce; store-
    bought, or see recipe page 214) or to taste

• Place noodles and bouillon in heat-safe bowl; add boiling water. Let stand, stirring occasionally, until noodles are softened and bouillon is dissolved, about 5 minutes.

• Drain noodles, pouring liquid into blender. Transfer noodles to serving bowl. Add remaining ingredients to blender and purée. Pour over noodles and toss.

Balsamic-Splashed Clementines

4 clementines or tangerines, peeled, sliced
    crosswise into 1/4-inch rounds, or 2 (81/2-ounce)
    cans mandarin oranges, drained

1 tablespoon balsamic vinegar

• Combine clementines and vinegar in a bowl; toss to coat.

Beach-Blanket Picnic

• "My Hero" Muffuletta • New Orleans Olive Salad • Melons in Mango Nectar • Hubba-Hubba 3-Lime Limeade

MAKES 4 SERVINGS

Pack a cooler and relax! Here's a day's worth of appetite-appeasing flavors to counter the salt-spray air.

GAME PLAN
1. Make salad.
2. Assemble sandwich.
3. Mix limeade. Pack melons.

"My Hero" Muffuletta

A muffuletta (or muffaletta) is a hero sandwich that originated in New Orleans in 1906 at the Central Grocery. Until you get to the Big Easy and have one there, you can enjoy this wherever you are.

1 (10- to 12-inch) round loaf Italian bread
New Orleans Olive Salad (recipe follows)
4 ounces thinly sliced ham or mortadella
4 ounces thinly sliced provolone cheese
4 ounces thinly sliced Genoa salami

• Cut bread in half horizontally; remove some of the soft insides, leaving enough to absorb the juice from the salad. Spread half the salad on the cut side of the bottom half of the bread; top with the ham, then the cheese, then the salami, and finally the remaining salad.

• Top with remaining bread half and press down firmly without squishing out the salad. Wrap tightly in plastic wrap; refrigerate up to 24 hours. To serve, cut into 4 wedges.

Note: A muffuletta can be eaten right after it's made but it is even better if made ahead so the bread can soak up the salad juices.

40

New Orleans Olive Salad

This tangy salad is what makes a muffuletta so distinctive. Try it on other sandwiches, especially turkey. The salad gets even better as it marinates.

2 cloves fresh garlic, crushed through a press
2 ribs celery, thinly sliced
1 (2-ounce) jar chopped pimientos, drained, or
   1/4 cup chopped roasted red peppers
1/2 cup imported black olives, pitted, slivered
1/2 cup green olives, pitted, slivered
1/4 cup pickled cocktail onions
1/4 cup good quality olive oil
2 tablespoons red-wine vinegar
2 tablespoons salted capers, rinsed
2 tablespoons torn fresh parsley leaves
1/2 teaspoon dried Italian seasoning or a mix of
   oregano and basil

• Mix ingredients together. Store in a glass jar.

Makes about 1 1/2 cups.

Melons in Mango Nectar

Melons and mangos are naturally cooling and thirst-quenching. Put them in a wide-mouth insulated container or pack in a cooler for transporting so they'll stay refreshing.

4 cups balls or 1-inch chunks assorted melons, chilled
1 (12-ounce) can mango nectar, chilled

• Combine melon and nectar in wide container or bowl so melons can soak in nectar.

Hubba-Hubba 3-Lime Limeade

juice of 3 limes
1 (6-ounce) can frozen limeade concentrate
1/2 cup bottled sweetened lime juice
crushed ice

• Mix ingredients with three limeade-concentrate cans of cold water. Add lots of crushed ice; pour into large insulated pitcher.

BUY TIME

Want a quicker salad? Drain 2 (9 3/4-ounce) jars of olive salad; place in bowl. Add 2 ribs celery, sliced, and 2 tablespoons torn fresh parsley; mix well.

A Taste of Distant Lands

• Curried Coconut Shrimp • Jasmine Rice
• Marinated Nectarines with Orange Flower Water

MAKES 4 SERVINGS

Steaming-hot crusty fried shrimp are hard to beat. Here they are tropicalized with fruit, coconut, and fragrant flowers.

GAME PLAN
1. Rinse and simmer rice.
2. Prepare nectarines.
3. Prepare shrimp.

Curried Coconut Shrimp

Since coconut gets top billing in this dish, it's worth it to use fresh coconut. Grate it a day or so in advance (store the meat in the refrigerator or freezer) or buy fresh frozen coconut or packaged finely grated, unsweetened coconut from an Asian grocery store.

2 pounds peeled, deveined jumbo shrimp, tails intact
4 tablespoons bottled sweetened lime juice
3/4 cup rice flour or all-purpose flour
1 tablespoon curry powder
2 eggs
2 cups fresh finely grated coconut, or packaged
  unsweetened coconut
vegetable oil for frying
bottled tamarind chutney for dipping (available from
  Indian grocery stores)

• Toss the shrimp with 2 tablespoons lime juice. Place flour and curry powder in plastic bag; add shrimp and toss to coat. Beat eggs with remaining lime juice in shallow bowl; place coconut on waxed paper. Dip shrimp in eggs to coat; drain off excess. Coat with coconut.

• Heat 1 inch oil in deep large skillet over medium-high heat until shimmering. Line a baking sheet with paper towels. In batches, fry shrimp until golden brown, about 1 minute per side. Drain on prepared baking sheet. Serve with chutney for dipping.

Note: If you can't find tamarind chutney, use bottled sweet and sour sauce or Chinese sweet chili sauce.

Jasmine Rice

1 cup jasmine rice
2 cups water

● Rinse rice in strainer. Combine with water in 2-quart saucepan. Heat to simmering over medium-high heat. Cover loosely; reduce heat and simmer 15 minutes.

● Remove rice from heat; fluff with fork. Cover; let stand 5 minutes.

Marinated Nectarines with Orange Flower Water

Gild the lily by serving this with ice cream, whipped cream, English double cream, mascarpone, or crème fraîche. So many choices—no problem when there's so little time!

4 large ripe nectarines, halved, pitted, thinly
*   sliced*
2 tablespoons sugar
1 teaspoon orange flower water (available at Italian
*   grocery stores)*
pinch of freshly grated nutmeg

● Mix ingredients in medium bowl. Let soak to soften, stirring occasionally, if time permits. Otherwise, spoon into goblets or glass bowls and serve.

A Dinnertime Dance of Flavors

• Seafood Fritters • Sambal Tartar Sauce • Plum-Glazed Flank Steak • Green Tea Noodles with Ginger Sauce

MAKES 4 SERVINGS

Here's a mix of sweet, sour, and spices playing off a juicy steak.

GAME PLAN

1. Heat water for noodles; preheat broiler. Glaze steak.
2. Broil steak. Make tartar sauce and fritter batter. Heat oil for fritters.
3. Cook noodles. Make ginger sauce. Fry fritters.

Seafood Fritters

vegetable oil for frying

1 cup corn-muffin mix

1/4 teaspoon Maryland-style seafood seasoning

1 egg, lightly beaten

1/3 cup milk plus more if needed

16 shucked oysters, clams, or mussels, coarsely chopped

kosher salt or fine sea salt to taste

lemon wedges for serving

Sambal Tartar Sauce (recipe follows) or bottled Chinese sweet chili sauce for dipping (optional)

• Preheat oven to 200°. Line a baking sheet with paper towels. Heat 1 inch oil in deep large skillet until shimmering (375° on a deep-fat thermometer.) Mix muffin mix and seafood seasoning in medium bowl; stir in egg and milk until smooth (do not overmix). Add shellfish; stir to mix.

• When a drop of batter dropped in the oil browns in 30 seconds, add tablespoonfuls of the fritter mixture (about 6 at a time). Fry until golden brown on one side, about 1 minute. Turn fritters and fry until golden brown on other side. Remove to prepared baking sheet and sprinkle lightly with salt. Keep warm in oven while frying remaining batter. Serve with lemon wedges and sauce.

BUY TIME

Make noodle sauce ahead; heat in pan used to cook noodles while noodles drain.

Sambal Tartar Sauce

1/2 cup mayonnaise

1 to 2 tablespoons fresh lemon juice

1 to 2 tablespoons Indian relish or other sweet pickle relish

1 teaspoon sambal oelek (Indonesian chili sauce; store-bought or see recipe page 214) or more to taste

● Mix mayonnaise with 1 tablespoon lemon juice, 1 tablespoon relish, and 1 teaspoon sambal oelek in a small bowl until blended. Taste and add more lemon juice, relish, and/or sambal oelek.

Plum-Glazed Flank Steak

1 pound flank steak

1/4 cup bottled Chinese plum sauce

1/2 teaspoon garlic salt or 1/4 teaspoon garlic powder or 2 cloves garlic, crushed through a press

● Preheat broiler; line broiler pan with foil. Score steak with 1-inch diagonal slashes in each direction on both sides. Place steak in pan; spread sauce on both sides (if using fresh garlic, mix with sauce before spreading). Sprinkle garlic salt on top side.

● Broil 4 inches from heat source 4 minutes on each side for medium-rare. Cover with foil; let stand 5 minutes before slicing across the grain.

Green Tea Noodles with Ginger Sauce

Bottled pickled ginger will add more of a sweet-and-sour flavor than fresh gingerroot.

8 ounces green-tea flavored soba noodles

1/4 cup vegetable oil

1/4 cup finely shredded bottled pickled ginger or peeled grated fresh gingerroot

3 tablespoons low-sodium soy sauce

1 1/2 teaspoons sugar

1/2 cup chicken broth

● Heat 2 quarts water in large deep skillet to boiling. Add noodles and return water to boiling. Add 1 cup cold water; return water to boiling and add 1/2 cup cold water. Boil again, add another 1/2 cup cold water and cook until al dente, 3 minutes (taste for doneness). Drain in strainer and rinse noodles with hot water. Set aside and keep warm.

● Heat oil in large wok or skillet over medium-high heat. Add ginger, soy sauce, and sugar; stir-fry 1 minute. Add chicken broth; heat to boiling, and stir-fry 2 minutes. Add noodles and remove pan from heat. Toss with wooden salad forks or chopsticks to coat noodles with sauce.

Some Enchanted Island Supper

• Croatian Cucumber Salad • Sizzling Squid with Garlic Butter • Spiced Plums with Agrodulce

MAKES 4 SERVINGS

With all of the stress and clamor that fill our days, it is a treat to be able to slide with ease into a charmingly delicious evening.

GAME PLAN
1. Simmer plums. Preheat broiler.
2. Make salad.
3. Cook squid.

Croatian Cucumber Salad

The artisanal cheeses from the little islands off the coast of Croatia are uniquely flavored because of the salt-water-misted grasses the sheep feed on.

1 English cucumber, halved lengthwise, seeded with
   a spoon, cut into 1/2-inch pieces
2 green onions, trimmed, chopped
1 cup chopped plum tomatoes or halved grape
   tomatoes
1/2 cup bottled Dijon vinaigrette
2 cups coarsely shredded aged Balkan sheep's milk
   cheese, kasseri, or ricotta salata

• Combine vegetables and vinaigrette in a salad bowl. Spoon into 4 deep soup bowls. Sprinkle each with cheese. Cover and refrigerate until serving.

Sizzling Squid with Garlic Butter

4 large cleaned squid
1 teaspoon salt
2 tablespoons unsalted butter
1 tablespoon extra-virgin olive oil
2 garlic cloves, crushed through a press
1 tablespoon chopped fresh parsley
2 tablespoons Italian-seasoned dried bread crumbs

• Preheat broiler. Cut squid tubes crosswise into 1/8- to 1/4-inch-thick rings. Sprinkle with salt and toss to coat.

• Melt butter in oil in large ovenproof skillet over medium heat. Add garlic and parsley and sauté 30 seconds. Add squid and sauté 1 minute. Sprinkle with bread crumbs and toss to coat. Broil about 4 inches from heat source just until lightly browned and sizzling, about 30 seconds.

Spiced Plums with Agrodulce

Ancient Roman cooks used agrodulce, a mixture of honey and vinegar, for everyday cooking and feasts as well. Here it makes simple plums shine.

2 tablespoons honey
2 tablespoons balsamic vinegar
2 tablespoons Cinzano or vermouth (red or white)
1 tablespoon unsalted butter
1/2 teaspoon ground cloves
1 (1-pound) can pitted plums, drained, or 1 pound
*   fresh Italian prune plums, quartered lengthwise,*
*   pits removed*
fennel seeds for garnish

• Heat honey and vinegar in medium skillet over medium heat until boiling. Add remaining ingredients except fennel seeds and cover. Cook, stirring occasionally to coat with flavorings, until plums are softened, 5 to 10 minutes. Sprinkle with fennel.

Supper for New Neighbors

• Cauliflower Soup with Creamy Pepper Cheese • Veal Piccata with Buttered Egg Noodles • Quick Babas au Rhum

MAKES 4 SERVINGS

Introduce yourself over a meal that's easy to assemble and suits all tastes.

GAME PLAN
1. Cook cauliflower. Soak babas. Heat water for noodles.
2. Coat veal scallops.
3. Finish soup. Cook noodles and veal. Glaze babas before serving.

Cauliflower Soup with Creamy Pepper Cheese

4 to 6 cups chicken broth
1 pound cauliflower florets
1 (5-ounce) package imported pepper-flavored soft cheese spread, in chunks
salt to taste
freshly ground pepper for serving

• Heat 4 cups broth to boiling in 2-quart saucepan; add florets and cook until soft, about 10 minutes. Remove florets to food processor using slotted spoon; add cheese spread and pulse until mixture is puréed, adding some hot broth through feed tube while processing if necessary.

• Whisk cheese mixture into broth in pan. Reheat without boiling. Taste and add salt and more broth as needed. Grind fresh pepper over each serving.

Makes 4 to 6 servings.

Veal Piccata with Buttered Egg Noodles

salt
2 lemons
1/4 cup all-purpose flour
1/2 teaspoon lemon-pepper seasoning
1/2 teaspoon garlic salt
1 to 1 1/2 pounds veal scallops
1 (8-ounce) package egg noodles
3 1/2 tablespoons unsalted butter
1 1/2 tablespoons olive oil
1/2 cup dry white wine
1 tablespoon torn fresh Italian parsley leaves
2 teaspoons drained small capers

• Heat 2 quarts salted water in deep large skillet to boiling. Grate 1 teaspoon zest from 1 lemon; squeeze juice and strain. Cut other lemon into wedges. Set aside. Mix flour, seasoning, and garlic salt on waxed paper. Coat scallops on one side with mixture; shake off excess.

• Cook noodles in boiling water until al dente. Meanwhile, melt 1 1/2 tablespoons butter in oil in large nonstick skillet over medium-high heat; when butter stops bubbling, add veal, floured side down, and cook until juice beads form on top, and bottom is golden, 1 to 2 minutes. Turn scallops over; cook until golden on other side, 1 to 2 minutes more. Remove to warm plate; drizzle with lemon juice. Cover loosely with foil; keep warm.

• Drain noodles; toss with remaining butter in a serving bowl. Keep warm. Add wine to hot skillet; boil over high heat until syrupy, stirring to clean pan. Stir in lemon zest, parsley, and capers; pour over veal. Serve with lemon wedges and noodles.

Quick Babas au Rhum

4 brioches or raisin muffins (not supersized)
3/4 cup bottled vanilla syrup (or see recipe, page 217)
1/4 cup dark Jamaican rum, or more to taste, and a little more for brushing
1 tablespoon apricot preserves, warmed in microwave, for brushing
4 candied cherries
finely chopped pistachios

• Prick muffins through several times with a thin skewer; place in pie plate.

• Heat syrup and rum in glass measure in microwave or in small saucepan until lukewarm. Pour over the babas; turn to soak. Let stand until serving, basting frequently with rum syrup. They should be moist and spongy but not wet enough to break up.

• To serve: Brush tops of brioches with warm preserves. Top with a cherry and sprinkle with nuts. Place in paper muffin liners on plates and serve.

Romantic Celebration

• Passion Fruit Kir Royales • Oysters in Herbsaint Sauce • Polenta Rounds • Chocolate-Covered Ice Cream Hearts • Raspberry Sauce • *Fresh Raspberries*

MAKES 2 SERVINGS

It doesn't have to be Valentine's Day or your anniversary to pull out all the stops for dinner. This elegant repast is trouble-free so you can relax over a toast and a smooch.

GAME PLAN

1. Make ice-cream hearts and freeze. Cut polenta into rounds.
2. Make raspberry sauce. Prepare oysters. Broil polenta.
3. At dessert time, pour sauce on plates; top with hearts and berries.

Passion Fruit Kir Royales

passion fruit liqueur

1 (25-ounce) bottle chilled sparkling wine

• Pour 1 to 2 teaspoons (eyeball it) of the liqueur into champagne flutes. Fill glasses with the wine.

BUY TIME

To slash prep time, look for presliced peppers in the grocery store produce department or salad bar.

Oysters in Herbsaint Sauce

1 pint shucked oysters, undrained

1/2 cup (1 stick) unsalted butter

4 thin slices prosciutto di Parma or Serrano ham or Smithfield ham, cut into 1/2-inch-wide strips

1/3 cup finely chopped shallots

1 cup mixed finely chopped green, yellow, and red bell peppers

2 tablespoons all-purpose flour

1/2 cup heavy cream

2 tablespoons Herbsaint (an anise-flavored New
    Orleans liqueur) or other anise-flavored liqueur
    such as Pernod, or more to taste
juice of 1 lemon (preferably a Meyer lemon) plus
    wedges for serving
Tabasco sauce to taste
freshly ground black pepper to taste
1 tablespoon finely chopped parsley

• Poach oysters in their liquor in a saucepan over medium heat until their edges curl. Remove from heat.

• In large skillet, melt butter over medium-high heat; sauté prosciutto until crisp, about 5 minutes. Remove prosciutto to a plate; keep warm. In buttery drippings, sauté shallots 3 minutes; sauté peppers 5 minutes; stir in flour and cook until fragrant, 1 minute. Stir in 1/2 cup oyster liquor; cook until boiling. Stir in cream, Herbsaint, lemon juice, Tabasco, and pepper; heat to boiling. Stir in oysters; heat through (do not overcook). Sprinkle with prosciutto and parsley.

Polenta Rounds

1 (24-ounce) tube prepared polenta
extra-virgin olive oil for brushing

• Preheat broiler. Line broiler pan with foil.

• Cut polenta into 1/2-inch-thick slices. Brush slices on both sides with oil; place in prepared pan. Broil 4 inches from heat, turning once, until browned, about 3 minutes per side.

Makes 4 to 6 servings.

Chocolate-Covered Ice Cream Hearts

2 (3/4-inch-thick) slices strawberry ice cream,
    gelato, or sorbet
1 (7-ounce) container chocolate ice-cream
    shell coating
4 heart-shaped candies with a message, 4 red
    cinnamon candies, or 1 tube decorating icing
    or gel
Raspberry Sauce (recipe follows)
fresh raspberries for serving

• Line a cookie sheet with parchment. Cut out 2 hearts from each slice of ice cream using a 3-inch heart cutter. Place on parchment. Freeze.

• Heat chocolate coating as package label directs, and pour over the hearts. Immediately place a candy in center of each heart or let chocolate harden and write your own message with decorating icing or gel. Serve immediately or freeze until serving. To serve: Pour sauce on plates and top with hearts and raspberries.

Raspberry Sauce

1 (10-ounce) package frozen red raspberries in
    syrup, thawed

• Purée raspberries and liquid in food processor; pass through strainer to remove seeds.

Makes about 1 1/4 cups.

April Fool's Dinner

• Oven-Fried Tofu "Chicken Nuggets" • Chutney Dipping Sauce
• Buttered Spaghetti-Squash "Noodles" • Apricot-Cream
"Fried Eggs" on Pound Cake "Toast"

MAKES 4 SERVINGS

It's hard to resist playing visual tricks with food on April Fool's Day. Here's a menu made for both flavor and fun.

GAME PLAN

1. Prepare tofu. Microwave spaghetti squash.
2. Make dipping sauce. Drain apricot slices on paper towels.
3. Butter cake slices; toast just before serving.

Oven-Fried Tofu "Chicken Nuggets"

nonstick cooking spray
1 pound firm tofu
1 cup seasoned bread coating mix for pork, chicken, or fish
Chutney Dipping Sauce (recipe follows)

• Preheat oven to 375°. Line a small baking sheet with foil; grease with cooking spray.

• Drain and rinse tofu; cut into 1-inch cubes. Place breading mix in plastic food storage bag; toss tofu cubes, a few at a time, in breading until coated. Place on baking sheet and bake until crisp, 10 to 15 minutes. Serve with dipping sauce.

Chutney Dipping Sauce

1 (15 1/2-ounce) jar mango chutney
1/2 cup dry white wine

• Pulse chutney and wine in blender or food processor until smooth.

5 4

Buttered Spaghetti-Squash "Noodles"

1/2 (3-pound) spaghetti squash, seeds scooped out
1/4 cup water
butter, salt, and pepper for serving

• Pierce squash on all sides with fork or metal skewer and place cut side up in glass baking dish. Add water to dish. Cover with microwave-safe plastic wrap; vent. Microwave on high power, turning dish every 4 minutes, until tender, 12 minutes. Let stand 5 minutes. Scoop out "spaghetti" with fork. Toss with butter and seasonings.

Apricot-Cream "Fried Eggs" on Pound Cake "Toast"

4 slices toasted buttered pound cake
1 cup sweetened whipped cream or mascarpone
  sweetened with honey
4 canned apricot halves, drained
ground allspice

• Place a slice of pound cake on a dessert plate. Top with a dollop of cream and spread gently to make an "egg-white" bed. Place an apricot half on top for the "yolk." Dust with allspice "pepper."

Not-Your-Ordinary Fish and Slaw Dinner

• Crispy Cornmeal Catfish Fillets • Preserved-Lemon Dipping Sauce • Savoy Cabbage Slaw

MAKES 4 SERVINGS

Anglers, awake! Flavors from afar infuse the traditional fish fry with élan and razzle-dazzle.

GAME PLAN
1. Make slaw.
2. Coat and fry fish.
3. Make dipping sauce.

Crispy Cornmeal Catfish Fillets

1/2 cup milk or water
3/4 cup cornmeal
1 teaspoon Maryland-style seafood seasoning
vegetable oil for frying
4 (8-ounce) thick catfish fillets
Preserved-Lemon Dipping Sauce (recipe follows)

• Place milk in a shallow bowl. In another shallow bowl combine cornmeal and seasoning. Heat about 1/8 inch of oil in large skillet over medium heat until simmering.

• Dip catfish fillets into milk to coat on both sides; drain off excess. Coat on both sides with cornmeal mixture; shake off excess.

• Fry fillets skin side down (if skin is on) in oil until browned and crisp, 3 to 4 minutes. Turn and fry on other side until browned and cooked through, 3 to 4 minutes more. Serve with dipping sauce.

Preserved-Lemon Dipping Sauce

3/4 cup water

2 tablespoons fresh lemon juice or more to taste

2 teaspoons cornstarch

2 teaspoons sugar or more to taste

2 tablespoons finely chopped preserved lemon
   (peel only; store-bought, or see recipe page 218)

1 tablespoon fresh cilantro leaves, torn

● Mix water, lemon juice, cornstarch, and sugar in a small saucepan until blended. Heat to boiling, stirring until clear and thickened. Stir in lemon peel and cilantro. Taste; adjust lemon juice or sugar as needed.

Savoy Cabbage Slaw

You can use bottled vinaigrette dressing instead of mayonnaise for a distinctive style of slaw.

1/2 cup mayonnaise

1/4 cup pesto (store-bought, or see recipe page 213)

1 small head Savoy cabbage

● Mix mayonnaise and pesto in a medium bowl. Quarter and core cabbage; cut wedges crosswise into thin shreds. Add cabbage to mayonnaise mixture and toss to coat.

Picnic on the Point

• Pan-Grilled Kielbasa on Kaiser Rolls • Pickled Onion and Mustard Topping • Russian Potato Salad

MAKES 4 SERVINGS

Watch the waterskiers and boats go by—or just imagine them—as you savor this tasty repast in your favorite park or backyard.

GAME PLAN

1. Heat water for kielbasa and vegetables. Make topping.
2. Blanch kielbasa. Cook vegetables.
3. Grill kielbasa. Toss salad.

Pan-Grilled Kielbasa on Kaiser Rolls

1¹/2 pounds kielbasa
6 kaiser rolls, split and toasted
Pickled Onion and Mustard Topping (recipe follows)

• Heat 1 quart water to boiling in shallow saucepan. Cut kielbasa into 4 equal pieces and halve lengthwise. Boil 2 minutes. Drain and rinse in colander.

• Heat grill pan or heavy skillet over medium heat until hot. Grill kielbasa cut sides down for 3 minutes. Turn with tongs 45° to make attractive grid lines if using a grill pan and grill 3 minutes. (If using a plain skillet, cook 6 minutes in all without moving.) Turn kielbasa and grill on skin side until skin is browned and ready to pop, about 3 minutes. Place in rolls and top with onion topping.

Pickled Onion and Mustard Topping

1 cup drained pickled cocktail onions, roughly chopped

3 tablespoons grainy prepared mustard

3 tablespoons sour cream

● Mix ingredients in small bowl.

Russian Potato Salad

1 (10-ounce) package frozen mixed vegetables

1 pound deli potato salad (from diced, not sliced, potatoes)

2 tablespoons Indian relish, or more to taste

● Cook vegetables as label directs; drain and rinse with cold water. Pat dry with paper towels and place in medium bowl. Add potato salad and relish and toss gently to mix. Taste, and add more relish if desired.

Retro Dinner Deluxe

• Cheese-Stuffed Mushrooms • Steak Diana/Diane • Pineapple Princess Salad

MAKES 4 SERVINGS

Americans emerged from our esoteric culinary legacy in the 60s and early 70s. We traveled abroad more, Julia Child had us fearlessly cooking French dishes, and we copied at home what was dazzling us in restaurants. The dishes that seemed to be the biggest trend were things served flaming: Crêpes, steaks, bananas, and even drinks were set on fire. Here's a groovy menu from that era of carefree exploration.

GAME PLAN

1. Preheat broiler. Prepare mushroom caps and filling.
2. Broil mushroom caps; fill and broil again. Prepare salad.
3. Cook steaks.

Cheese-Stuffed Mushrooms

Once upon a time in America, fresh mushrooms were unavailable in the hinterlands except to knowledgeable foragers. Wow. Think about that as you scarf down these simple-to-make succulent appetizers!

1 pound (1-inch-diameter) fresh mushrooms, cleaned
extra-virgin olive oil for drizzling
1 (5-ounce) package imported pepper-flavored soft
  cheese spread, at room temperature
1 cup dry herb-stuffing mix

• Preheat broiler. Line broiler pan with foil.

• Remove stems from mushrooms. Place in prepared pan; drizzle with oil. Broil 4 inches from heat source until hot, about 5 minutes.

• Mix cheese spread and stuffing in bowl; spoon into mushroom caps. Broil until bubbly, about 5 minutes. Serve hot.

Steak Diana/Diane

The presentation here is adjusted to serve four instead of the usual one: Instead of flaming the steak in the pan, a flaming sauce is poured over the steaks on the platter. Oh yes: Diana was a Greco-Roman goddess of the forest and therefore is identified with deer. Embrace your neighborhood hunter and invite him or her in for a feast!

4 (10-ounce) thin well-trimmed boneless venison or
  beef sirloin steaks, at room temperature
salt and freshly ground pepper to taste
6 tablespoons unsalted butter
1/2 cup dry sherry
2 tablespoons snipped fresh chives
1/4 cup Cognac or brandy

● Place steaks between sheets of plastic wrap. With the flat side of a meat mallet or a rolling pin, *gently* pound meat to 1/4-inch thickness. Season steaks on both sides with salt and pepper.

● Melt 2 tablespoons butter in large skillet over medium-high heat. Add 2 steaks and brown on both sides, about 4 minutes in all. Remove to warm platter; cover them with foil to keep warm. Repeat with 2 tablespoons butter and remaining steaks.

● Add sherry to pan; stir, scraping up browned bits. Boil 2 minutes. Pour into a small saucepan. Transfer steaks to clean, warm, oven-safe platter; sprinkle with chives and place on the table. Add any juices from steaks and remaining butter to saucepan and swirl without boiling until melted. Add Cognac and heat without boiling. Carefully ignite, using a long-handled match. Immediately pour over steaks and serve.

Pineapple Princess Salad

This is an updated version of a salad that was just as delicious in its original iceberg incarnation.

4 clean leaves butterhead or Boston lettuce
4 round slices peeled, cored fresh pineapple or
  4 canned pineapple rings
freshly ground pepper to taste
4 dollops mayonnaise (aioli, wasabi, bacon, chipotle,
  European-style, or plain)
1/2 cup shredded extra-sharp cheddar cheese or other
  favorite cheese

● Place lettuce leaves on plates; top with pineapple rings. Sprinkle with pepper. Dollop mayonnaise in centers of rings; sprinkle with cheese.

Feast on the Riviera

• Sweet-Vermouth Floats • Tuna Niçoise Sandwiches • Plums with Chèvre and Lavender Sugar

MAKES 4 SERVINGS

The light, the people, the water, the food. A day on the Mediterranean coast enters the brain and never leaves. Eat in an everlasting daydream.

GAME PLAN

1. Make sandwiches.
2. Assemble plum desserts and chill.
3. Assemble floats just before serving.

Sweet-Vermouth Floats

1 cup sweet red vermouth (such as Dubonnet),
  chilled
1/2 pint lemon sorbet or gelato
orange-peel twists

• Pour vermouth into 4 short glasses. Dollop in sorbet using a melon-ball scoop. Garnish with orange twists. Serve with short straws.

Tuna Niçoise Sandwiches

With a little artistic license, the components of the classic Niçoise salad come together inside a crusty loaf of bread.

2 (18-inch) French baguettes
extra-virgin olive oil
1/4 cup tapenade (olive paste; store-bought, or see recipe page 215) or sliced pitted imported olives
1 European cucumber, thinly sliced
1 cup deli egg salad
4 marinated sun-dried tomatoes, slivered
1 (6-ounce) can solid white albacore tuna (water- or oil-packed), drained, flaked
freshly ground pepper to taste
freshly squeezed lemon juice to taste
anchovy fillets (optional)

● Cut the breads in half lengthwise but not all the way through, making the bottom half slightly thicker than the top; remove most of the soft insides. Drizzle oil inside of top; spread tapenade over cut side of bottom half. Arrange a thin layer of cucumber over tapenade. Spread egg salad on top; sprinkle with tomatoes. Scatter tuna over tomatoes; season well with pepper and lemon juice. Arrange a line of anchovies down the center.

● Press down hard on the sandwich without squeezing out the egg salad. Cut each sandwich crosswise into 4 sections using a serrated knife.

Plums with Chèvre and Lavender Sugar

If you'd like to use Italian prune plums, you will want to serve two or three per serving.

4 ripe plums
4 ounces young chèvre
fresh mint sprigs
1 tablespoon dried lavender flowers
1/4 cup sugar

● Halve plums; remove stones. Place plum halves cut sides up on dessert plates.

● Fill center of each plum half with a dollop of cheese. Gently press halves together to reassemble plums. Insert a mint sprig in the stem end of each plum.

● Crush lavender with sugar in a mortar; sprinkle over plums.

"Bring on the Belly Dancers" Dinner

• Ground Lamb Kebabs • Yogurt-Dill Sauce
• Couscous with Fiddlehead Ferns and Mushrooms

MAKES 4 SERVINGS

Lamb has an exotic culinary legacy associated with a wide range of flavors. Here, it is simply seasoned and served with a classic yogurt sauce and an unusual orange-enhanced couscous. Now, where did you put those finger cymbals?

GAME PLAN

1. Preheat broiler or grill. Assemble kebabs and begin broiling or grilling.
2. Blanch fiddleheads; turn skewers. Finish couscous.
3. Turn skewers; make dill sauce. Turn skewers.

Ground Lamb Kebabs

Grill these over charcoal at your next barbecue.

1 pound ground lamb
1 small onion, minced, plus extra for serving
1 garlic clove, minced
1 egg white, lightly beaten
1 tablespoon sweet or hot paprika
1 teaspoon salt
extra-virgin olive oil for greasing skewers and pan
lemon wedges, small Italian hot pickled peppers
    (pepperoncini), and Yogurt-Dill Sauce (recipe
    follows) for serving

• Preheat broiler or prepare gas or charcoal grill. Combine lamb, onion, garlic, egg white, paprika, and salt in a large bowl; knead with your hand into a paste. Roll into 1-by-2-inch sausage shapes, wetting hands lightly to keep meat from sticking.

• Brush 4 long metal kebab skewers with oil; thread "sausages" through short sides onto skewers, allowing 1/4 inch between pieces and using a dampened hand to gently squeeze meat against skewers to attach firmly.

• Line broiler pan with foil and brush with oil or brush grill rack with oil. Brush skewers with oil and arrange in broiler pan or on grill rack. Broil or grill kebabs 4 inches from heat source, turning every 2 minutes, until browned and crisp on all sides, about 10 minutes in all. Serve with minced raw onion, lemon, peppers, and Yogurt-Dill Sauce.

Yogurt-Dill Sauce

1 cup plain Greek-style whole-milk yogurt

big pinch of garlic powder or 1 large garlic clove,
crushed through a press

1 tablespoon dried dill weed or 1/4 cup snipped
fresh dill

pinch of salt

- Combine ingredients in bowl and mix well.

Couscous with Fiddlehead Ferns and Mushrooms

You can use asparagus instead of the fiddleheads; the flavors are surprisingly similar.

1 3/4 cups water

1/2 teaspoon salt or to taste

8 ounces fresh fiddlehead ferns

1 1/2 cups couscous

4 ounces sliced mushrooms (any kind)

4 tablespoons unsalted butter, in small pieces

2 tablespoons torn flat-leaf parsley leaves

1 tablespoon grated orange zest (optional)

- Bring water to boiling in small saucepan; add the salt and fiddleheads and boil 1 minute. Remove fiddleheads with slotted spoon to a bowl of ice water.

- Add couscous, mushrooms, and butter to water. Stir, cover, and remove from heat. Drain ferns and add to couscous. Fluff with fork. Let stand at least 5 minutes.

- Taste couscous and adjust salt if needed. Spoon into serving dish; sprinkle with parsley and orange zest.

Dad's (or Kids') Night to Cook

• One Minute Steak and Tomato Stew • Garlic-Chive Mashed Potatoes • Raisin Bread and Buttermilk Pudding Parfaits

MAKES 4 SERVINGS

Here's a foolproof dinner that will satisfy those with robust appetites coming in from a Saturday of yard work or relaxing after the ballgame.

GAME PLAN

1. Assemble parfaits; refrigerate.
2. Make stew.
3. Mix potatoes.

One Minute Steak and Tomato Stew

The steak is a prime cut, so it takes only a minute to cook. For everyday budgets, you can use any cut of thinly sliced boneless beef—and even pork, lamb, chicken, turkey, or venison. The cooking time will be a little longer, but it's still a quick-cook dish.

3 tablespoons olive oil

1 large onion, thinly sliced

1/4 teaspoon salt or more to taste

1/8 teaspoon freshly ground black pepper

1 green bell pepper, seeded and sliced
   lengthwise into 1/2-inch pieces

2 teaspoons dried oregano

1/8 teaspoon crushed red-pepper flakes

1 1/2 pounds boneless sirloin steak, cut into 1/4-inch-
   thick slices or thinner

1 (16-ounce) can peeled whole tomatoes
   (preferably San Marzano), drained, juices
   reserved, tomatoes coarsely chopped

• Heat oil in a large skillet or dutch oven over medium-high heat. Add onion, salt, and pepper. Cover; cook 3 minutes. Add green pepper, oregano, and pepper flakes. Stir-fry 2 minutes. Add beef; stir-fry 1 minute. Add tomatoes and their juice and heat to boiling.

Garlic-Chive Mashed Potatoes

*1 (1 1/4-pound) pouch refrigerated mashed potatoes,
heated, or 4 cups hot prepared instant or leftover
mashed potatoes*
*1/4 cup snipped garlic chives or 1 teaspoon crushed
garlic and 1/4 cup snipped regular chives*
salt and pepper to taste

● Combine potatoes and chives in serving bowl.
Season to taste.

Raisin Bread and Buttermilk Pudding Parfaits

You can use 1 cup granola instead of making the
bread crumbs.

*2 slices raisin-pumpernickel bread or cinnamon-
raisin bread, toasted*
2 cups buttermilk or fruit-flavored yogurt smoothie
1/2 cup vanilla yogurt
ground cinnamon for dusting

● Tear bread into pieces and pulse in food processor
until even, 1/4-inch crumbs form.

● Spoon half the crumbs and then half the smoothie
into 4 serving bowls or parfait glasses; repeat. Add a
dollop of yogurt on top. Refrigerate. Just before serving, sprinkle with cinnamon.

Combo of Complementary Contrasts

• Chilled Blue Cheese and Pear Soup with Radicchio
• Broiled Fennel and Shrimp Panini

MAKES 4 SERVINGS

Here's a soup and sandwich match-up that's special enough for company. The lively flavors, colors, and textures make for so interesting a meal, all you need for dessert is a bite of that chocolate you've been hoarding. Use a pointed cheese knife, such as the kind used for digging out wedges of Parmigiano-Reggiano, to break up a large chunk of chocolate.

GAME PLAN

1. Preheat broiler and sandwich grill. Make soup.
2. Broil shrimp and fennel.
3. Assemble and grill sandwiches.

Chilled Blue Cheese and Pear Soup with Radicchio

1 (16-ounce) can pear slices in natural juices

1/2 cup sour cream

1/4 cup bottled sweetened lime juice

2 cups ice water

freshly grated nutmeg to taste

1 cup shredded radicchio

1/4 cup crumbled blue cheese

• Drain pears, reserving juice. Cut pears into 1-inch chunks and pulse in food processor, adding juice as needed, until pears have an even, chunky texture (1/4- to 1/2-inch pieces).

• Pour pears into a large bowl and whisk in remaining pear juice, the sour cream, and lime juice. Add ice water. Season with nutmeg. Ladle into bowls and sprinkle with radicchio and blue cheese.

Broiled Fennel and Shrimp Panini

1/4 cup balsamic vinaigrette (store-bought, or see
recipe page 215)
4 baby fennel bulbs, trimmed, halved lengthwise
8 large shelled, deveined shrimp, halved lengthwise
1 teaspoon fresh thyme leaves (no stems)
4 ciabatta rolls
2 tablespoons extra-virgin olive oil
5 ounces chèvre (goat's milk cheese), crumbled

- Preheat broiler. Line broiler pan with foil and brush with a little of the vinaigrette. Arrange fennel and shrimp, cut sides up, in pan. Brush with vinaigrette and broil 4 inches from heat for 2 minutes. Turn, brush with remaining vinaigrette, and sprinkle with thyme. Broil until shrimp are pink and barely cooked through, about 2 minutes. Remove shrimp to a plate. Broil fennel until tender, about 1 minute. Remove to plate with shrimp.

- Slice ciabattas horizontally into thirds. Brush the cut sides of tops and bottoms with oil; broil until browned, 1 minute. Reserve middle slices for another use. Arrange fennel, shrimp, and cheese on bottoms; cover with tops. Press in a skillet or sandwich grill until browned, 3 minutes. Serve warm or at room temperature.

Taste of Spring

• Fresh Pea Soup • Roasted Lamb Salad in Rice Paper Rolls • *Lemon Gelato with Bakery Cookies*

MAKES 4 SERVINGS

Peas, mint, and lamb: It must be spring! Here's an ideal meal to serve on newly scrubbed patio furniture.

GAME PLAN
1. Make soup.
2. Preheat broiler. Cook lamb.
3. Assemble rice paper rolls.

Fresh Pea Soup

Use a ten-ounce package of frozen peas if you can't find fresh peas.

4 cups water or broth
1 cup shelled fresh peas
1/2 cup soft garlic and herb-flavored cheese
salt to taste
yogurt thinned with milk for drizzling
fresh mint sprigs for garnish

• Heat water in small saucepan to boiling. Add peas and cook just until tender, 2 to 3 minutes.

• Carefully purée water, peas, and cheese in blender, in batches so mixture doesn't overflow. Pass through a food mill or sieve into a bowl. Season with salt if needed. Ladle into bowls, drizzle with yogurt, and garnish with mint.

Roasted Lamb Salad in Rice Paper Rolls

1 1/2 *pounds boneless leg of lamb, sliced*

1/2 *cup balsamic vinaigrette (store-bought, or see*
   recipe page 215)

8 Vietnamese rice paper wrappers

8 leaves butter or Boston lettuce

1 cup fresh cilantro leaves

1 star fruit (carambola), slivered

low-sodium soy sauce mixed with rice vinegar to
   taste, for dipping

● Preheat broiler. Arrange lamb slices between 2 sheets of plastic wrap. Pound with a rolling pin or mallet to 1/8-inch thickness. Line broiler pan with foil; brush with some vinaigrette. Place lamb slices on top; brush with some vinaigrette. Broil 4 inches from heat source until sizzling, about 1 minute each side. Pour cooking juices into a bowl. Cut lamb into thin strips and toss with juices.

● To serve: Soak wrappers in a bowl of hot water for 5 to 10 seconds; pat dry. Place on work surface. Place a lettuce leaf in center of each. Top with lamb, cilantro, and star fruit. Fold one end over filling and fold sides over as you would for a burrito. Serve with dipping sauce.

Eclectic Soup and Sandwich Dinner

• Vietnamese Beef and Noodle Soup • Fruit and Cheese Sandwiches • *Lemongrass Tea*

MAKES 4 SERVINGS

A hearty bowl of soup needs just a little rounding out to call it a meal. Here, the classic trio of bread, fruit, and cheese fit the bill.

GAME PLAN

1. Heat stock and water for noodles.
2. Sauté walnuts and fruit; assemble sandwiches.
3. Cook and drain noodles; heat beef in soup.

Vietnamese Beef and Noodle Soup

Serve this soup with a showy presentation: Bring the bowls with hot noodles and lettuce to the table and ladle in the broth and beef from a tureen.

8 cups beef stock or broth
10 to 12 ounces thinly sliced deli roast beef, cut crosswise into 1/4-inch strips (about 2 cups)
1 pound fresh rice-stick noodles or Hong Kong noodles, or 6 ounces (4 bundles) cellophane noodles
1 small head Bibb or Boston lettuce, leaves separated, rinsed, torn into quarters
vegetable oil or dark sesame oil for drizzling

Vietnamese or Thai fish sauce (nuoc mam or nam pla) for serving
Chinese chili sauce, sambal oelek (store-bought, or see recipe page 214) or other red chili sauce for serving

• Heat stock to boiling in a large saucepan. Heat 1 1/2 quarts water to boiling in another saucepan.

• Add beef to stock and reduce heat to simmer. Add noodles to boiling water; stir with chopsticks to separate. Cook until tender. Drain noodles and place in deep soup bowls. Add lettuce; drizzle with oil.

• Transfer broth with meat to a tureen. To serve: Add broth and beef to soup bowls at the table; pass fish sauce and chili sauce for guests to season soup to taste.

76

Fruit and Cheese Sandwiches

4 tablespoons unsalted butter

1/4 cup chopped walnuts

1 large Granny Smith apple, cored, thinly sliced

1 large Bartlett pear, cored, thinly sliced

1/2 cup bottled chutney

4 (6-inch) pieces (no "heels") thin French baguette

8 ounces ripe Brie (or Fontina Valdostana, rind removed), cut into thin slices

4 ounces blue cheese, crumbled

● Melt butter in large skillet over high heat; add nuts and sauté until fragrant, 1 minute. Add fruit; sauté until tender and juices evaporate, about 5 minutes. Stir in chutney; remove from heat.

● Slit open baguette pieces on one side; remove a little of the soft insides. Line bottom halves with Brie; top with fruit mixture and sprinkle with blue cheese. Squeeze gently to hold filling ingredients inside bread.

Trophy Winners' Celebration Feast

• Veal Chops Milanese • Quick Tomato Coulis • Two-Tone Tartufi

MAKES 4 SERVINGS

Oh, to bask in the glow of victory! Whatever the challenge—academic, athletic, or economic—heartfelt cheers and spirited toasts can be happily shared with the victors over a juicy chop dinner and some disguised ice cream for dessert.

GAME PLAN
1. Make and freeze tartufi.
2. Make coulis.
3. Coat chops and cook.

Veal Chops Milanese

1/2 cup all-purpose flour
1 cup coarsely shredded Parmigiano-Reggiano cheese
1 cup fine dried bread crumbs
2 eggs
4 (1/2-inch-thick) veal rib chops, rib bones "frenched" by the butcher
salt and freshly ground pepper to taste
4 tablespoons unsalted butter
1/4 cup olive oil
Quick Tomato Coulis (recipe follows)

• Place flour in a shallow dish. Mix cheese and crumbs in another shallow dish. Lightly beat eggs in a third shallow dish. Season chops well with salt and pepper, dredge in flour, then egg, and then cheese mixture, lightly pressing coating into chops.

• Melt butter in oil in a large skillet over medium-high heat. Cook chops until golden on one side, 3 to 4 minutes. Turn the chops and fry the other side until cooked through, 5 to 6 minutes more. (Make sure the oil does not get too hot, so the chops do not brown too quickly.) Serve with the coulis.

Quick Tomato Coulis

The trendy use of the word coulis (pronounced koo-LEE) on restaurant menus can refer to anything and everything from a thick purée to a cold relish to a sauce. That's OK—it's good to be flexible.

1 (14.5-ounce) can diced tomatoes with chilies
2 tablespoons torn fresh parsley or mint

● Drain tomatoes; reserve juice. Pulse tomatoes quickly in food processor so that some are puréed but there are chunks, too, adding enough reserved liquid to make it the desired texture. Heat or chill as desired. Stir in parsley before serving.

Makes 4 to 6 servings.

Two-Tone Tartufi

These Italian truffles are cold and sweet surprise packages. You can serve them in a pool of raspberry or chocolate sauce and no one will protest.

1 pint chocolate gelato
1 pint coffee gelato
4 whole toasted almonds or hazelnuts
4 maraschino cherries or amarene (Italian cherries in heavy syrup), drained
1 (7-ounce) container chocolate ice-cream shell coating

● Line a small baking sheet with parchment. Scoop 2 equal-size balls (they do not have to be perfectly round or smooth) of each flavor gelato and place on parchment. Working quickly so the gelato will not melt, cut balls in half. Press 1 almond and a cherry into the center of 1 chocolate half. Press a coffee half onto the chocolate half, smearing the overflow so the ball is smooth. Repeat with remaining halves to make 4 two-tone balls. Freeze at least 10 minutes.

● Remove gelato balls from freezer. Heat chocolate coating as package label directs and pour enough over gelati balls to coat completely. The coating should harden almost instantly. Serve immediately or freeze until serving.

Spice Caravan Kebab Dinner

• Spicy Lamb Kebabs • Apricot-Cinnamon Kasha • Beet and Blood Orange Salad

MAKES 4 SERVINGS

Here's a meal for the armchair traveler waiting to realize reservations or reveling in memories.

GAME PLAN

1. Soak skewers. Marinate lamb.
2. Cook kasha. Assemble salad.
3. Grill kebabs.

Spicy Lamb Kebabs

1/4 cup pesto (store-bought, or see recipe page 213)

1/4 cup Spanish or other fruity olive oil

1/4 cup fresh lemon juice

1/2 teaspoon ground cumin

1/2 teaspoon hot paprika

2 pounds lean boneless lamb (from the leg), cut into thin, 1-inch-wide strips

salt to taste

lemon wedges for serving

• Soak 4 wooden skewers in water. Combine pesto, oil, lemon juice, cumin, and paprika in shallow bowl; mix well. Add lamb; mix with your hands, gently rubbing the marinade into the meat. Thread meat onto

BUY TIME

If you want to save time and buy lamb already cubed, it will make fine kebabs, only the chunks will not absorb the marinade as much as would strips. Marinate in half the marinade; then baste the kebabs with remainder during cooking. Do not overcook.

skewers so that each slice is skewered in 2 places to hold it secure. Let stand at least 10 minutes or refrigerate overnight.

• Prepare gas or charcoal grill or preheat broiler. Line broiler pan with foil if using broiler. Grill or broil kebabs 4 inches from heat source, turning frequently, until meat is nicely crisp, about 5 minutes. Sprinkle with salt; serve with lemon wedges for squeezing to taste.

Apricot-Cinnamon Kasha

3 tablespoons olive oil

1 large red onion, chopped

1 cup whole kasha

1 1/2 teaspoons ground cinnamon

2 1/2 cups vegetable or chicken broth or water

1/2 cup dried apricots, coarsely chopped

salt to taste

• Heat oil in a large skillet over medium-high heat. Add onion, kasha, and cinnamon; sauté until onion starts to soften, about 3 minutes. Add broth and apricots; heat to boiling. Reduce heat and simmer, mostly covered, until kasha is softened, about 10 minutes. Taste and adjust salt if needed.

Makes 4 to 6 servings.

Beets and Blood Orange Salad

3 blood oranges

1 tablespoon Dijon mustard

2 teaspoons red-wine vinegar

salt and freshly ground pepper to taste

1/3 cup grapeseed oil

1 (1-pound) can sliced beets, drained

8 paper-thin crosswise slices from a red onion

1 (4-ounce) log young chèvre (goat's milk cheese), rolled in herbs

• Cut peel off oranges using a small serrated knife over a large bowl to collect the juices. Cut oranges crosswise into 1/3-inch-thick rounds on a cutting board that has a trough around the edges. Place the oranges in a small bowl; pour juices in trough into bowl with juice. Add mustard, vinegar, salt, and pepper to juice; whisk until blended. Whisk in oil in a thin steady stream until thickened. Taste and adjust seasonings.

• Add beets, oranges, and onion to dressing; toss to mix and separate onion into rings. Place on plates.

• Crumble chèvre on top of salads.

BUY TIME

Use 1 cup bottled grapefruit sections or citrus salad instead of cutting the oranges.

Every Day Is New Year's by the Bayou

• Seared Scallops with Andouille Sausage • Hoppin' John (Black-Eyed Peas with Rice) • Uppity Collards

MAKES 4 SERVINGS

A traditional New Year's meal in the American South combines cooked greens, which signify paper currency, and beans, which signify coins, to ensure prosperity in the months ahead. But hide your zydeco CDs until after this dinner: With one taste of the spicy Louisiana andouille sausage, guests will want to leap up and dance!

GAME PLAN

1. Start rice. Cook collards and sauté pancetta.
2. Brown scallops and sausage. Mix collards and pancetta.
3. While scallops poach, mix peas and rice.

Seared Scallops with Andouille Sausage

2 tablespoons unsalted butter

1 tablespoon vegetable oil

16 to 20 medium sea scallops, patted dry

4 ounces andouille sausage or other spicy hard sausage, thinly sliced

1/4 cup dry white wine or white vermouth

1 (8-ounce) container sour-cream dip with vegetables

1/4 cup torn or shredded fresh basil leaves

• Melt butter in oil in large nonstick skillet over medium-high heat. Add scallops and cook until browned on each side, about 1 minute in all (do not cook through). Remove to plate and keep warm. Add sausage to pan and sauté until browned, about 3 minutes.

• Add wine to skillet; stir, scraping up browned bits. Add scallops and simmer to reduce wine to a glaze, 1 to 2 minutes. Stir in dip and heat to simmering over medium heat. Cover pan. Simmer to barely poach scallops through, about 4 minutes. Sprinkle with basil.

Hoppin' John (Black-Eyed Peas with Rice)

1 cup rice
2 1/2 cups water
1 tablespoon unsalted butter
1 (16-ounce) can black-eyed peas
1 teaspoon Tabasco sauce
1 small bunch green onions, trimmed, thinly sliced crosswise

● Rinse rice. Combine water, rice, and butter in a 2-quart saucepan. Heat to boiling over medium heat; reduce heat and simmer until rice is almost tender but still slightly wet, about 15 minutes.

● Drain and rinse peas. Gently stir peas and Tabasco into rice with wooden salad fork. Heat through. Sprinkle with green onions.

Uppity Collards

Smoked ham or bacon is traditionally used to season full-flavored collard greens. Here, pancetta, an unsmoked Italian bacon, adds a touch of class.

1 (10-ounce) package frozen chopped collard greens
2 to 3 ounces pancetta, chopped
1/8 teaspoon freshly ground black pepper

● Thaw and cook collards as package label directs. Meanwhile, sauté pancetta in a medium skillet over medium heat until all fat is rendered and pancetta is crisp, about 10 minutes.

● Using tongs or slotted spoon, transfer collards to pan with pancetta and toss. Moisten as desired with collard green cooking liquid. Season with pepper.

A Dinner That's Amore!

• Melon and Prosciutto Salad • Welsh Rarebit, Italian-Style • Chocolate-Dipped Pizzelles

MAKES 4 SERVINGS

Here's a pasta-less menu that's full of flavors, textures, and colors that are trademarks of Italian food.

GAME PLAN

1. Make cheese sauce; keep warm.
2. Dip pizzelles. Toss salad.
3. Toast bread.

BUY TIME

Cut-up or sliced cantaloupe is usually available in grocery store produce departments or salad bars.

Melon and Prosciutto Salad

4 ounces mesclun salad mix

2 cups diced cantaloupe

6 ounces thinly sliced prosciutto or other ham, cut into 2-inch pieces

1/3 cup red-wine vinaigrette (store-bought, or see recipe page 216)

• Combine mesclun, melon, and ham in salad bowl. Drizzle with dressing; toss.

Welsh Rarebit, Italian-Style

The English version of this classic open-faced cheese sandwich combines beer and Cheshire cheese. This recipe is a cross between bruschetta and a French fondue. If you can't find imported fontina, use your imagination! A Vermont or other cheddar and a local wine or microbrewed beer will make a mix worthy of praise.

4 tablespoons unsalted butter
1 tablespoon all-purpose flour
1/2 cup white wine, preferably Italian
1/2 cup whole milk, half-and-half, or heavy cream
1 pound Italian fontina cheese (not domestic),
  shredded
4 thick diagonal slices crusty country-style
  Italian bread
1 garlic clove, cut in half
1/4 teaspoon white pepper or to taste
wedge of Parmigiano-Reggiano cheese

• Melt butter in a heavy saucepan over medium heat and stir in flour. Cook until bubbly and golden. Remove from heat and gradually whisk in wine and milk until smooth. Heat to boiling. Gradually whisk in the fontina, stirring in one direction only.

• When the fontina has melted and the mixture is very hot, toast the bread. Rub one side of each slice with the garlic and place toast in shallow bowls. Taste cheese mixture, add pepper if needed, and pour over toasts. Sprinkle with shavings of Parmigiano-Reggiano.

Chocolate-Dipped Pizzelles

1/2 cup colored sprinkles or sugar
1/2 cup chocolate chips
4 Italian pizzelle cookies or crisp Italian ladyfingers

• Place sprinkles in shallow bowl. Melt chocolate chips in another shallow bowl in microwave. Dip edges of pizzelles into chocolate and then the sprinkles. Place on parchment-lined baking sheet and refrigerate until chocolate is set.

Leisurely Poolside Breakfast for Dinner

• Primarily Peach Smoothies • Hangtown Fry (Oyster Omelet) • *Thick Slices of Toast* • Chutney Glazed Broiled Fruit

MAKES 4 SERVINGS

The fresh clear water and bright reflected sunlight is like a scene from Miami Vice. Why dine inside when you can live large and get your toes wet?

GAME PLAN
1. Preheat broiler. Assemble kebabs.
2. Make smoothies. Fry oysters and start omelet.
3. Broil kebabs. Make toast.

Primarily Peach Smoothies

1 (8-ounce) can pineapple chunks in natural juices
2 cups frozen peaches
2 cups strawberry yogurt
1 seedless orange, peeled, chopped
ground allspice for dusting
4 strawberries with hulls

• Reserve four pineapple chunks; pour remainder and juices into blender. Add peaches, yogurt, and orange; blend on high speed until smooth. Pour into glasses; dust with allspice. Impale a pineapple chunk and then a strawberry on each of four long skewers; place one in each glass to garnish.

Hangtown Fry (Oyster Omelet)

This legendary combination comes from the Old West tradition that a man was allowed his favorite foods before he went to the gallows.

9 large eggs
1 cup cracker crumbs
8 to 12 large oysters, shucked
3 tablespoons water
1 (7-ounce) jar chopped pimientos, drained
2 tablespoons snipped fresh chives
salt and freshly ground pepper to taste
6 tablespoons unsalted butter, softened
8 to 12 bacon strips, fried until crisp

● Beat one egg in a bowl. Place cracker crumbs on a plate. Dip oysters in egg to coat; drain off excess. Roll in crumbs to coat.

● Beat remaining eggs with water, pimientos, chives, salt, and pepper until well blended.

● Melt butter in very large nonstick skillet over medium-high heat. Add oysters and fry until golden. Add egg mixture and cook as you would an omelet, dragging cooked egg to center of pan so uncooked portion runs underneath. Make sure oysters are evenly distributed. When omelet is set but not dry, slide out onto a hot platter. Garnish with bacon.

Chutney Glazed Broiled Fruit

3/4 cup bottled chutney
1/4 cup fresh lemon juice
1 kiwifruit, unpeeled, quartered lengthwise
1 firm banana, peeled, cut into 1-inch pieces
1 seedless orange, unpeeled, quartered
8 (1-inch) chunks fresh pineapple
2 slices cantaloupe, cut into 1-inch chunks
2 slices honeydew, cut into 1-inch chunks

● Preheat broiler. Line broiler pan with foil. Mix chutney with lemon juice. Impale some of each type of fruit on skewers. Place in prepared pan and brush with chutney glaze. Broil 4 inches from heat source, turning several times and brushing with glaze, until hot, about 5 minutes.

"Too Lazy to Go Out" Dinner Brunch

• Blood-Orange Sunrises • Two-Pepper Cheese Fondue • Marsala Chicken Liver Sauté • *Scrambled Eggs*

MAKES 4 SERVINGS

It's five o'clock and you're still in pajamas. The fridge is full—you've even got chicken livers to cook up!

GAME PLAN
1. Make fondue. Make sunrises.
2. Sauté livers.
3. Scramble eggs.

Blood-Orange Sunrises

8 tablespoons apricot or peach nectar
1 quart blood-orange juice

• Pour 2 tablespoons nectar into each of 4 fluted glasses. Holding a tablespoon right side up over nectar, pour in juice, allowing it to trickle from the bowl of the spoon into the glass. (This will keep the colors separate.)

Two-Pepper Cheese Fondue

1 (17-ounce) jar Alfredo sauce

1/2 to 1 cup milk

1 (7-ounce) jar chopped pimientos, drained

2 canned chipotles in adobo sauce, chopped, or more
    to taste

sliced fresh fruit (apples, pears, peaches, etc.),
    radicchio leaves, blanched vegetables, pretzels,
    toast points, cooked shrimp, etc., for dipping

• Whisk sauce, 1/2 cup milk, pimientos, and chipotles in a large nonstick skillet over medium heat until boiling; add enough extra milk to make coating consistency. Transfer to a serving dish on an electric hot plate or a fondue pot over canned heat and keep warm. Have guests dip at their leisure.

Makes 4 to 6 servings.

Marsala Chicken Liver Sauté

1 pound chicken livers, trimmed

1/4 cup rice flour or all-purpose flour

1/2 teaspoon onion salt or celery salt

1/2 teaspoon lemon-pepper or lemon-herb seasoning

2 tablespoons unsalted butter

2 tablespoons vegetable oil

1 large shallot, finely chopped

1/3 cup Marsala or sherry (dry, amontillado,
    or cream)

1 cup half-and-half, or 1/2 cup heavy cream plus
    1/2 cup chicken broth

1/4 cup chopped fresh parsley

2 tablespoons drained capers

• Rinse livers; pat dry. Mix flour, onion salt, and seasoning in plastic food storage bag. Add livers and shake to coat.

• Melt butter in oil in large skillet over medium-high heat. Add livers and sauté until browned on the outside but pink inside, 3 to 4 minutes. Remove to a warm platter; cover with foil.

• Sauté shallot in drippings until softened, about 2 minutes. Add Marsala; stir, scraping up browned bits. Add half-and-half; simmer 5 minutes. Taste; adjust seasoning if needed. Return livers to skillet; heat through. Sprinkle with parsley and capers.

Gravlax Revisted with a Kiss of the Tropics

• Little Smoked Salmon Frittatas • Chinese Mustard and Sesame Sauce • Warm Coconut Rice Pudding

MAKES 4 SERVINGS

The flavors of gravlax, the Swedish specialty of salmon cured with dill, salt, and sugar, inspire this tasty egg dish. A spiced-up version of the classic mustard sauce completes the tribute. And a comforting rice pudding has the flavors of a Nordic vacation.

GAME PLAN

1. Start rice. Prepare wok or steamer.
2. Make frittatas and steam.
3. Make sauce.

Little Smoked Salmon Frittatas

8 eggs
3 tablespoons water
big pinch of garlic powder
4 ounces Nova Scotia smoked salmon bits or
  chopped sliced smoked salmon
2 green onions, trimmed, finely chopped
2 tablespoons torn fresh cilantro leaves
nonstick cooking spray
Chinese Mustard and Sesame Sauce (recipe follows)

• Prepare wok or steamer with simmering water. Break eggs into bowl; add water and garlic powder. Whisk until smooth but not frothy. Stir in salmon, onions, and cilantro.

• Grease 4 custard cups with cooking spray; divide egg mixture evenly among cups. Place cups in wok or on steamer rack over simmering water. Cover cups with a sheet of foil. Cover and steam gently until eggs are set and a knife inserted in center comes out clean, 10 to 15 minutes. Cool slightly before running a knife around edges of each; invert onto plates. Serve with mustard sauce.

Chinese Mustard and Sesame Sauce

2 tablespoons black sesame seeds

2 tablespoons white sesame seeds

1/2 cup imported Dijon mustard

2 tablespoons dark sesame oil

1/2 teaspoon bottled sweetened lime juice or sugar
   to taste

1 to 2 tablespoons hot water

• Heat seeds in small skillet over medium heat, stirring, until very fragrant. Pour into bowl; whisk in mustard, oil, and lime juice. Thin to desired consistency with hot water.

Warm Coconut Rice Pudding

1 cup sticky (sweet or sushi) rice or regular
   long-grain rice

1 (13.5-ounce) can unsweetened coconut milk

1/2 cup lime or orange marmalade plus extra,
   melted, for garnish

1/2 cup tropical mix dried-fruit blend, diced, for
   garnish (optional)

• Rinse rice; place in 2-quart saucepan. Add coconut milk; rinse out can with half a canful of water and add to rice. Heat to boiling over medium heat and add marmalade. Reduce heat and simmer, covered, until rice is tender, 15 minutes. Set aside until serving.

• To serve: Spoon rice pudding into individual bowls; drizzle with melted marmalade. Sprinkle with fruit mix.

Feeling-of-Summertime Dinner

• Smothered Pork Chops with Mixed Peppers
• Steamed Corn on the Cob • Basil Butter

MAKES 4 SERVINGS

The fresh flavors and aromas of a garden harvest are packed into this menu. It's a worthy inspiration for a visit to the farmers' market.

GAME PLAN
1. Sauté onion; purée roasted peppers.
2. Prepare corn for steaming. Brown chops.
3. Make onion-pepper sauce; steam corn. Make Basil Butter.

Smothered Pork Chops with Mixed Peppers

You can use sliced fresh bell peppers (1 cup total red, green, and yellow) instead of the pickled peppers. Sauté them a few minutes with the onion.

2 tablespoons unsalted butter

1 tablespoon olive oil

1 (8-ounce) sweet onion, thinly sliced

1 (7-ounce) jar roasted red peppers

1 teaspoon dried oregano

1/4 teaspoon garlic salt

4 (1/2-inch-thick) boneless pork chops (5 ounces each)

4 small pickled hot red cherry peppers

4 small pickled hot green cherry peppers

1/2 cup red or white wine

1/2 cup chicken broth or water

• Melt butter in oil in large nonstick skillet over medium-high heat. Sauté onion until tender, 7 minutes. Meanwhile, purée (undrained) roasted peppers with oregano and garlic salt in food processor; set aside.

• Remove onion to plate using slotted spoon. In same pan, brown pork chops on both sides, 3 minutes in all. Add puréed pepper mixture, onion, cherry peppers, wine, and broth. Simmer gently over medium heat until chops are cooked through, about 4 minutes.

Steamed Corn on the Cob

You can season the ears of corn with Basil Butter before rolling them up in plastic wrap. If the butter is hard, just cut off bits and dot them over the corn.

4 ears corn, shucked, or 8 frozen (3-inch) ears corn
Basil Butter (recipe follows)

• Rinse corn; place each wet ear of corn horizontally facing you on a sheet of microwave-safe plastic wrap. Fold bottom of plastic around ears; fold over ends of wrap and roll up, egg-roll style. Cook ears together in microwave on high power 5 minutes. Let stand in plastic until ready to serve. Serve with butter.

Note: Corn can also be cooked in saucepan of boiling water for 3 to 5 minutes.

Basil Butter

1/2 cup (1 stick) butter, cut into small chunks
6 large fresh basil leaves, or more to taste
salt and freshly ground pepper to taste

• Combine butter, basil, salt, and pepper in food processor; pulse until blended. Taste for seasoning. Scrape into 4 egg cups for serving.

Midsummer Sunday Meal Inspired by Vera

• Avocado and Smoked Salmon Appetizer • Pan-Fried Duck Breast with Cherry Sauce • Broiled Asparagus • *Unhulled Strawberries and Double Cream for Dipping*

MAKES 4 SERVINGS

My friend Vera and her beloved dogs live in a cottage north of London. On a recent visit there, I was dazzled by the resplendent summer Sunday meal she prepared. This is a hurried-up interpretation of it. To make radicchio leaf cups, simply peel off leaves of the head of the radicchio and layer them, creating small cups.

GAME PLAN

1. Score and cook duck; start sauce. Preheat broiler.
2. Prepare appetizer without avocado. Broil asparagus.
3. Finish duck and sauce. Slice avocados. Wash berries just before serving.

Avocado and Smoked Salmon Appetizer

4 (1/8-inch-thick) slices smoked salmon
radicchio leaf cups
2 cups deli cole slaw with mayonnaise
2 ripe but firm avocados, halved, pitted, peeled

• Without driving yourself crazy, fold salmon slices in half and curl loosely into a cone. Place on large chilled plates. Place radicchio cups near salmon. Add coleslaw to cups using a fork to lift slaw to drain slightly. Slice avocados lengthwise; fan out on empty spots on plates.

Pan-Fried Duck Breast with Cherry Sauce

For an all-cherry sauce, you can use the juice from bottled cherries or a carton of cherry juice instead of the wine and brandy.

2 boneless duck-breast halves (2 pounds total), excess
*   fat removed, patted dry*
kosher salt and freshly ground black pepper

SAUCE

1 cup chicken stock (from bouillon is OK)

4 whole cloves

1 shallot, chopped

1/4 teaspoon ground mace

1/2 cup port wine plus 1 to 2 tablespoons kirschwasser
(cherry brandy) or 1/2 cup red wine plus 1 to 2
tablespoons cherry liqueur

2 teaspoons cornstarch

1 cup fresh, bottled or frozen, thawed and pitted
Bing cherries

salt, pepper, and fresh lemon juice to taste

● Score skin side of breasts, 1/4-inch deep, in a 1/2-inch crisscross pattern. Sprinkle liberally with salt and pepper and rub over duck.

● Heat a heavy large skillet over medium heat. Place breasts skin side down in pan. Cook, basting meat with hot fat to cook from top and adjusting heat so skin doesn't burn, until fat is rendered and skin is browned, about 10 minutes. Turn breasts over and cook 4 minutes longer for medium-rare. Remove to cutting board; cover and let rest at least 5 minutes.

● While duck cooks, make sauce: Combine stock, cloves, shallot, mace, wine, and 1 tablespoon brandy or liqueur in small saucepan. Heat to boiling over medium-high heat; reduce heat to medium and simmer 10 minutes. Strain sauce into a glass measure; discard solids. Clean saucepan; add remaining 1 tablespoon brandy or liqueur and cornstarch and blend. Whisk in sauce; heat to boiling, whisking until

thickened. Stir in cherries; heat through. Add salt, pepper, and lemon juice to taste.

● To serve: Thinly slice duck breasts across the grain. Fan out slices on plates. Spoon sauce around slices.

Broiled Asparagus

You can peel and cook asparagus ends when you have more time, but when you're in a hurry just place the bunch on the cutting board and whack off the last 3 inches in one fell swoop.

2 (1-pound) bunches asparagus, ends trimmed

2 tablespoons olive oil

salt and freshly ground pepper to taste

● Preheat broiler. Line a large shallow roasting pan with a sheet of foil.

● Spread asparagus in parallel lines in prepared pan; sprinkle with oil, salt, and pepper. Toss to coat. (Keep spears parallel.) Broil 4 inches from heat source, for 4 minutes; turn spears. Broil until asparagus is tender, for 3 to 5 minutes longer.

Girls Gone Wild! Bridesmaids' Bounty

• Seabreeze Punch • Cherry Cheese Blintzes • *Omelets to Order* • Grilled Chocolate Sandwiches

MAKES 6 SERVINGS

Take time out before the wedding to honor the bride-to-be with a memorable meal and lots of laughs.

GAME PLAN

1. Preheat oven. Assemble sandwiches; freeze.
2. Make blintzes; keep warm in oven. Make punch.
3. Grill sandwiches. Make omelets to order.

Seabreeze Punch

1 quart grapefruit juice

1 1/2 cups cranberry juice cocktail

1 cup vodka, or to taste (optional)

crushed ice

• Combine ingredients in punchbowl or pitcher. Stir to mix.

Makes 6 to 8 servings.

Cherry Cheese Blintzes

2 cups fresh ricotta cheese

2 egg yolks

1/4 cup undrained Italian cherries, marinated in brandy syrup, plus extra for garnish

12 store-bought or homemade (8- or 9-inch) crêpes

2 to 3 tablespoons unsalted butter

unsweetened cocoa powder and confectioners' sugar for dusting

freshly grated nutmeg

mint sprigs

crème fraîche or mascarpone for serving

• Preheat oven to 200°. Mix cheese, egg yolks, and cherries and their syrup in a bowl. Drop about 3 tablespoons in the center of each crêpe. Fold two facing sides of crêpe over the filling and roll up from one end.

• Melt butter in large skillet over medium-high heat. In batches, fry blintzes on both sides cooking on folded-up side first, until crisp and golden brown. Keep fried blintzes warm on baking sheet in oven while frying remaining blintzes.

• To serve: Dust plates with cocoa powder. Place blintzes on top, and dust with confectioners' sugar. Sprinkle with nutmeg and cherries and spoon syrup on tops. Garnish with mint and serve with crème fraîche.

Makes 4 to 6 servings.

Grilled Chocolate Sandwiches

8 slices of plain white bread (artisan to supermarket all work; yield depends on the dimensions of the bread)

1/2 cup chocolate-hazelnut spread

handful of chocolate chips

1 to 2 tablespoons unsalted butter, softened

• Coat one side of four pieces of bread with hazelnut spread. Press about 2 teaspoons of chocolate chips into the center area only.

• Spread softened butter over one side of the remaining slices of bread. Place one slice, buttered side up, over each chocolate-spread slice and press lightly around the edges to seal. Freeze 5 to 15 minutes.

• Heat a griddle over medium heat and cook the sandwiches first on the unbuttered side until lightly toasted, about 1 minute. Turn over the sandwiches and weigh them down with a baking pan with 2 to 3 pounds of weight. Toast the sandwiches until golden, 1 minute longer.

• Cut sandwiches in half diagonally.

Makes 4 sandwiches, 4 to 8 servings.

Al Fresco Supper

• Bruschetta with Tapenade • Tuna and White Bean Salad • Limoncello-Laced Strawberries

MAKES 4 SERVINGS

Practice your *per favore* and *grazie* as you glory in a traditional Italian repast on the terrace.

GAME PLAN

1. Preheat broiler. Marinate berries.
2. Assemble salad.
3. Make bruschetta.

Bruschetta with Tapenade

2 cups diced fresh or drained canned tomatoes

2 tablespoons shredded fresh basil

salt and freshly ground pepper to taste

1 (1-pound) loaf Italian bread, cut into 3/4-inch thick diagonal slices

1/3 cup tapenade (olive paste; store-bought, or see recipe on page 215) or pesto (store-bought, or see recipe on 213)

• Preheat broiler. Mix tomatoes, basil, salt, and pepper in bowl. Place bread on baking sheet. Broil 4 inches from heat source until toasted on both sides. Spread tapenade on one side of each slice of toast. Top with tomatoes and juices.

Tuna and White Bean Salad

4 ounces mesclun salad mix

2 (8-ounce) cans imported tuna in oil, drained

1 (19-ounce) can cannellini beans, drained and rinsed

2 plum tomatoes, chopped

1/2 cup chopped red onion

1 Kirby cucumber, chopped

2 tablespoons torn fresh Italian parsley leaves

salt and freshly ground black pepper to taste

extra-virgin olive oil for drizzling

1 lemon, cut into wedges, for serving

● Arrange mesclun on 4 plates. Top with tuna, beans, vegetables, and parsley. Sprinkle with salt and pepper. Drizzle with oil and serve with lemon wedges.

Limoncello-Laced Strawberries

2 pints ripe strawberries, hulled, halved

1/2 cup limoncello (Italian lemon liqueur)

freshly ground pepper to taste

● Gently toss berries with liqueur and pepper in bowl. Spoon into compote glasses.

Hearty and Eclectic Dinner

• *Brandade* of Alder-Smoked Salmon • Miso Soup with Broiled Tofu and Asian Greens • Mulled Crimson Pears

MAKES 4 SERVINGS

This repast will enlarge your world through your palate. A few select ingredients will inspire you to mix them in new ways.

GAME PLAN
1. Heat broth for soup. Simmer pears.
2. Preheat broiler. Make *brandade*.
3. Broil tofu; add to soup.

Brandade of Alder-Smoked Salmon

Dried salt cod is the basis of the classic French appetizer *brandade de morue*; here, the flavors of the Pacific Northwest find their niche in the potato medium. Substitute smoked trout, country ham, or even pitted imported olives for the salmon, if you're so inclined.

8 ounces alder-smoked salmon, in 1-inch pieces
1 cup warmed leftover potatoes, or 1 cup from a (1 1/4-pound) pouch of refrigerated mashed potatoes, or 1 cup prepared instant or leftover mashed potates
1/4 teaspoon garlic powder or 1 clove garlic, crushed through a press
1/4 cup fruity olive oil
salt and freshly ground pepper to taste
2 tablespoons snipped fresh chives
croûtes (small rounds of toasted baguette) or crackers

• Combine salmon, potatoes, and garlic powder in a food processor and pulse until blended. With machine running, pour in oil and process until just blended. Season to taste. Spoon into a shallow serving bowl or individual dishes and sprinkle with chives. Serve with croûtes.

Miso Soup with Broiled Tofu and Asian Greens

6 cups water

6 tablespoons white miso paste

2 tablespoons roasted-garlic teriyaki sauce or
   soy sauce

2 Japanese leeks or 4 green onions, cleaned, julienned

2 cups mizuna or watercress leaves

1 baby bok choy, shredded into 2-by-1/2-inch pieces

2 (3-ounce) squares firm tofu

oil for brushing

● Preheat broiler. Heat water, 4 tablespoons miso, and the terikayi sauce to boiling in a large deep skillet; add vegetables. Simmer while preparing tofu.

● Pat tofu dry with paper towels. Slice each piece horizontally into 3 pieces. Pat dry again. Line a baking sheet with foil and brush with oil.

● Thin remaining miso to coating consistency with a little warm water; brush over both large sides of tofu slices. Broil, 4 inches from heat source, turning once, until fragrant. Cut each square into 9 equal squares. Add to soup and serve.

Mulled Crimson Pears

1 (1-pound) can pear slices in heavy syrup

1 cup sweet red vermouth (such as Dubonnet)

mint sprigs for garnish

● Drain pears and place in single layer in skillet. Add vermouth. Heat to boiling over medium heat; simmer, basting occasionally, until evenly tinted, about 10 minutes. Remove from heat; boil vermouth until reduced by half, to concentrate the flavor. Pour over pears; garnish with mint sprigs.

A Special Duck Dinner

• Pan-Fried Glazed Duck Breasts • Saffron Rice with Pomegranate Seeds and Green Onions • Pistachio Parfaits

MAKES 4 SERVINGS

Dazzle the gourmand and artist with this scrumptious and colorful array of easily prepared dishes. Keep it to yourself that it wasn't hard to make!

GAME PLAN
1. Score and cook duck.
2. Cook rice. Baste ducks.
3. Assemble parfaits without topping; freeze.

Pan-Fried Glazed Duck Breasts

2 boneless duck-breast halves (2 pounds total),
   excess fat removed, patted dry
2 tablespoons maple or other syrup (fruit,
   corn, etc.)
2 tablespoons soy sauce
kosher salt and freshly ground black pepper to taste

• Score skin side of breasts 1/4-inch deep in a 1/2-inch crisscross pattern. Mix syrup and soy sauce; rub over duck. Sprinkle liberally with salt and pepper and rub in.

• Heat a heavy large skillet over medium heat. Place breasts skin side down in pan. Cook, basting meat with hot fat to cook from top and adjusting heat so skin doesn't burn, until fat is rendered and skin is browned, about 10 minutes. Turn breasts over and cook 4 minutes longer for medium-rare. Remove to cutting board; cover and let rest at least 5 minutes.

• To serve: Thinly slice duck breasts across the grain. Fan out slices on plates.

Saffron Rice with Pomegranate Seeds and Green Onions

1 cup rice

1/2 teaspoon saffron threads

1 tablespoon unsalted butter

1 teaspoon salt

2 cups hot water

1 small bunch green onions, trimmed, thinly sliced crosswise

1/2 cup pomegranate seeds

• Rinse rice. Crush saffron in 2-quart saucepan with back of spoon. Add butter, salt, and hot water. Stir rice into saffron mixture; heat to boiling over medium-high heat. Stir once; reduce heat to medium-low and simmer 10 minutes.

• Add green onions to rice; gently stir with wooden salad fork. Cover; cook until rice is tender, 5 minutes. Gently stir pomegranate seeds into rice.

Pistachio Parfaits

8 tablespoons bottled grenadine syrup or chocolate sauce (homemade or store-bought)

1 pint pistachio or vanilla ice cream, slightly softened

aerosol whipped-cream topping or sweetened whipped cream

chopped pistachios for sprinkling

• Spoon 2 tablespoons syrup or sauce into each of 4 parfait glasses or champagne flutes. Add 2 half-scoops of ice cream to each and press down gently with the back of a spoon so the syrup oozes between the chunks of ice cream. Top with dollops of topping and sprinkle with pistachios.

Note: To make ahead, assemble the parfaits without the topping up to 3 hours before serving and freeze. To serve, let stand at room temperature just long enough to soften the ice cream, and garnish with the topping and pistachios.

Wikiwiki Luau

• Macadamia-Crusted Crab Cakes • Baby Greens with Pineapple Vinaigrette • Big Kahuna Coconut Snowballs • Kona Mocha Sauce

MAKES 4 SERVINGS

It takes days of preparation for a true luau, or "feast" in Hawaiian. But you can have a fabulous mainland version if you wikiwiki ("hurry up"). Put on your flowered shirt, improvise some leis, and get ready to eat and hula!

GAME PLAN
1. Make crab cakes. Make snowballs.
2. Make sauce. Make salad.
3. Fry crab cakes; serve on salad.

Macadamia-Crusted Crab Cakes

It may take a relaxed island mindset to keep the heat under these cakes to a minimum. Just focus on gently browning them and they will be perfect.

1 pound lump crabmeat

4 slender green onions, trimmed, finely chopped

2 tablespoons finely chopped pickled ginger

2 tablespoons fresh lemon juice

2 egg whites

1 cup macadamia nuts, finely chopped

2 tablespoons unsalted butter

2 tablespoons peanut oil

• Gently pick over crabmeat for shells, placing clean pieces in medium bowl as you check. Add onions, ginger, and lemon juice. Beat egg whites until frothy; pour half into crab mixture. Stir gently with chopsticks to mix. Form into 4 (1-inch-thick) cakes using 2 icing spatulas. Brush with remaining egg white; pat on nuts. Turn over; repeat. Cover and refrigerate until frying.

• Melt butter in oil in heavy nonstick skillet over medium heat. Cook crab cakes until nuts are toasted, about 5 minutes. Turn and repeat. Remove to warm plate.

Baby Greens with Pineapple Vinaigrette

Although baby greens are perceived as better than their more mature counterparts because they are so tender, they can also be bland. Taste them to make sure they are juicy and vibrantly flavored.

1/4 cup canned or fresh crushed pineapple
3 tablespoons cider vinegar
pinch of garlic powder
salt and freshly ground pepper to taste
1 (8-ounce) bag mesclun salad mix

● In a large serving bowl, whisk together pineapple, vinegar, garlic powder, salt, and pepper. Add greens; toss to coat.

Big Kahuna Coconut Snowballs

The tiny, rice-like shreds of coconut found in Asian grocery stores allow for total snowy coverage of the ice cream, but you can use regular shredded coconut.

1 cup finely grated Asian-style coconut or sweetened,
*   shredded coconut, toasted*
1 pint coconut ice cream or gelato
Kona Mocha Sauce (recipe follows)

● Spread coconut over a dinner plate. Scoop ice cream into 4 equal-size balls; roll each in coconut to thickly coat. Serve immediately or place on a parchment-lined baking sheet, cover, and freeze until ready to serve. Serve with mocha sauce.

Kona Mocha Sauce

1/2 cup unsweetened cocoa powder
1/2 cup sugar
1/2 cup double-strength brewed Kona or other coffee
1/2 cup crème fraîche
2 tablespoons coffee-flavored liqueur (optional)

● Mix cocoa and sugar in small saucepan. Whisk in coffee. Heat to boiling over medium-high heat, whisking constantly. Boil 1 minute, continuing to stir. Remove from heat.

● Whisk crème fraîche and liqueur in bowl; whisk in hot syrup. Serve warm or at room temperature (do not boil if reheating) with ice cream, fruit, or cake.

Makes about 1 1/2 cups.

BUY TIME

Use pineapple ice-cream topping or preserves instead of canned or fresh. Thin with a little hot water or melt in the microwave for a few seconds for a coating consistency.

Grecian Quail Fit for the Gods

• Homemade Pita Chips with *Taramosalata* • Broiled Mint-Basted Quail • Fig and Arugula Salad

MAKES 4 SERVINGS

These blissful little bites will have you pining for sunny days on the Aegean. If you can't find the Greek taramosalata (a creamy fish-roe spread), dip those pita chips in some hummus instead, by Zeus!

GAME PLAN
1. Preheat broiler. Make pita chips.
2. Assemble salad. Make mint sauce.
3. Broil quail.

Homemade Pita Chips with *Taramosalata*

Flavorful pita wedges are perfect for dipping in taramosalata, a creamy Greek specialty made from coral-colored carp roe.

2 thin pocketless pita breads or 2 regular pita breads, halved horizontally
1/4 cup vinaigrette or Caesar salad dressing (store-bought, or see recipes pages 216 and 217)
1 (12 1/2-ounce) jar of taramosalata

• Preheat broiler. Brush pitas on both sides with vinaigrette. Stack pitas; cut crosswise in half. Stack halves and cut stacks into 4 wedges. Spread out wedges in single layer on baking sheet. Broil 6 inches from heat source until sizzling, 2 to 3 minutes. Turn over wedges and repeat. Pitas will crisp up as they cool. Serve with taramosalata for dipping.

Broiled Mint-Basted Quail

8 semi-boneless quail, pinions and second wing
   joints removed
1/2 cup imported mint jelly with mint leaves, or
   1/2 cup regular mint jelly plus 1/4 cup chopped
   fresh mint leaves
1/4 cup olive oil
1/4 teaspoon garlic salt or powder
1/4 teaspoon lemon-pepper seasoning

• Preheat broiler. Place quail in foil-lined baking pan.

• Combine jelly, oil, garlic salt, and seasoning in a
small heat-safe bowl. Cover with microwave-safe
plastic wrap and microwave on high power until jelly
melts, 2 minutes. Stir to blend. (Jelly can also be
melted in a small saucepan over medium-high heat.)

• Brush one-half of the mint sauce over quail; broil
quail skin side up 4 to 5 inches from heat source until
skin is browned and crisp, about 3 minutes. Turn with
tongs, brush with remaining sauce, and broil on second side until quail are cooked through and browned,
about 3 minutes.

Fig and Arugula Salad

4 cups arugula leaves
8 ripe fresh figs (Black Mission figs are ideal),
   quartered
1/4 cup citrus vinaigrette (store-bought, or see recipe
   page 216) plus more if needed

• Combine arugula and figs in salad bowl. Drizzle
with dressing and toss to coat. Add more dressing if
needed.

Twilight Supper under Swaying Palm Trees

• Grilled Fish Packets • Fresh Fruit and Sweet-Onion Salad • Tostones (Twice-Fried Plantains)

MAKES 4 SERVINGS

Whether you have palm trees or not, this menu will transport most any venue into a tropical paradise.

GAME PLAN

1. Preheat broiler or prepare grill. Make salad.
2. Assemble fish packets; cook. Fry plantains.
3. Flatten plantains; fry a second time.

Grilled Fish Packets

You can cook chicken-breast fillets, boneless pork, shrimp or even tofu in packets, too. These fillets are simply seasoned to allow the flavors of succulent fresh fish to emerge.

4 (6- to 8-ounce) snapper, flounder, sole, halibut or
    sea bass fillets
2 tablespoons Spanish or other fruity olive oil or
    flavored oil
1 tablespoon fresh lime juice
8 leaves fresh basil, torn into rough shreds
salt and freshly ground pepper to taste

• Prepare charcoal grill or preheat broiler. Place each fillet on a sheet of foil. Sprinkle with oil, lime juice, basil, salt and pepper. Seal foil around fish.

• Place packets directly on hot coals or oven rack; grill or broil until fish is cooked through, 12 to 15 minutes. The fish is eaten from the packets.

Fresh Fruit and Sweet-Onion Salad

1 small Maui or other sweet onion, coarsely chopped

2 cups fresh pineapple chunks, chopped

1 pint fresh strawberries, hulled, quartered
   lengthwise

1 Asian pear or Granny Smith apple, cored,
   coarsely chopped (optional)

1/4 cup torn fresh mint leaves

2 tablespoons fresh lemon juice

2 tablespoons olive oil or flavored oil

1/2 teaspoon freshly ground white or black pepper
   or more to taste

- Mix ingredients in medium bowl.

Makes 4 to 6 servings.

BUY TIME

Use 1 (16-ounce) can crushed pineapple in natural
juices, drained, instead of fresh pineapple.

Tostones (Twice-Fried Plantains)

2 green plantains

vegetable oil or peanut oil for frying

4 garlic cloves, peeled, halved lengthwise

salt to taste

- Cut the plantains crosswise in half; cut off the ends. Make four lengthwise slits at equal intervals around each half through the skin just to the flesh. Peel off each section of skin. Cut plantains into 3/4-inch rounds.

- Heat 1 inch oil in large skillet over medium-high heat. When the oil is hot enough to sizzle when a plantain round touches it, fry as many rounds as will fit in the pan without crowding. Cook until light brown, about 2 minutes; turn with a slotted spoon and brown other side. (Adjust heat if necessary.) Drain on paper towels. Repeat with remaining plantains. Remove skillet from heat. You can do the second frying now or set aside the skillet and plantains until ready to serve.

- Place a plantain between 2 sheets of parchment; crush it firmly with the heel of your hand or with a rolling pin to an 1/8-inch thickness. Repeat with remaining plantains. Add garlic to hot oil or reheat oil until hot (about 375°) over medium heat. Remove garlic when it starts to brown. Fry plantains in batches, turning until rich golden color. Drain on paper towels. Sprinkle with salt.

Sweet-and-Sour Chicken and Rice

• Tamarind-Marinated Chicken Breasts • Kaffir-Lime Pilaf • Wine-Poached Dates with Crème Fraîche

MAKES 4 SERVINGS

It's a big world out there, with millions of ingredients to explore. You can experiment with several new ones here and get to feel comfortable with their personalities.

GAME PLAN
1. Start rice. Marinate chicken.
2. Poach dates.
3. Cook chicken. Reduce date syrup.

Tamarind-Marinated Chicken Breasts

The sour flavor of tamarind calls for a bold blend of other ingredients as a countermeasure.

MARINADE
8 fresh basil leaves
1/2 cup fresh cilantro leaves
1/4 cup Thai or Vietnamese fish sauce (nam pla or nuoc mam)
2 tablespoons tamarind paste (available at Indian grocery stores)
2 tablespoons vegetable oil
1 tablespoon ground coriander
1 teaspoon Tabasco sauce
1/2 teaspoon garlic salt

1 pound thin chicken cutlets
1/4 cup water
salt and pepper to taste
4 green onions, trimmed, thinly sliced crosswise

• Pulse marinade ingredients in food processor until smooth, adding a little water if needed; spread over both sides of chicken pieces. Let stand 10 minutes.

• Heat water in a nonstick skillet over medium-high heat. Add the chicken and marinade; cover and cook 3 minutes. Turn the chicken and cook until done, for 3 more minutes.

• Transfer chicken to plates. Stir cooking juices and season with salt and pepper; pour over chicken. Sprinkle with green onions and serve.

Kaffir-Lime Pilaf

1 cup jasmine rice, rinsed

2 cups vegetable or chicken broth

4 kaffir lime leaves (available at Thai grocery stores)
*   or 1 lime, cut in half*

● Combine ingredients in 2-quart saucepan. Heat to boiling over medium-high heat, stir once and cover. Reduce heat to medium-low and gently simmer until rice is tender, 15 minutes. Let stand 5 minutes. Remove lime leaves or halves.

Wine-Poached Dates with Crème Fraîche

2 cups red wine

1 envelope spiced apple-cider mix or 2 tablespoons
*   sweetened spiced-tea mix ("Russian Tea")*

8 medjool dates

1/4 cup crème fraîche

cinnamon for dusting

● Heat wine and cider mix to simmering in 2-quart saucepan. Add dates, cover and poach gently over medium-low heat until puffed, about 5 minutes. Remove dates to bowl with slotted spoon; remove skins and pits. Place dates on dessert plates.

● Boil wine mixture until reduced by half, about 5 minutes; drizzle over dates. Garnish each plate with a dollop of crème fraîche and a dusting of cinnamon.

Fiesty Fish-Cake Dinner

• Sambal Salmon Cakes • Lemongrass Dipping Sauce • Peas-and-Carrots Noodle Salad

MAKES 4 SERVINGS

These are not your grandmother's salmon patties! The vivid and vibrant Asian ingredients will have your mouth sizzling—but begging for more.

GAME PLAN

1. Blanch peas and soak noodles. Make salad dressing.
2. Mix salmon mixture; shape cakes.
3. Fry cakes. Make dipping sauce.

Sambal Salmon Cakes

1 (16-ounce) can sockeye salmon

12 saltine crackers

1 egg, lightly beaten

2 teaspoons sambal oelek (Indonesian chili sauce; store-bought or see recipe page 214)

1 tablespoon unsalted butter

1 tablespoon vegetable oil

Lemongrass Dipping Sauce (recipe follows)

• Pour salmon and its juices into a bowl; remove skin and large bones. Crush crackers into the bowl. Add egg and sambal oelek; gently mix with fork. Shape into 8 (3/4-inch-thick) patties.

• Melt butter in oil in nonstick skillet over medium heat. Fry cakes on both sides until golden and crisp, adjusting heat as necessary, about 8 minutes in all. Drain on paper towels. Serve with dipping sauce.

Lemongrass Dipping Sauce

2/3 cup vegetable broth, fish stock, or water

2 tablespoons minced lemongrass (tender
   insides only)

1 tablespoon minced chives or green onion

1 tablespoon low-sodium soy sauce

1 teaspoon cornstarch

1/2 teaspoon sugar

salt to taste

• Combine ingredients in small saucepan until blended. Heat to boiling, stirring until clear and thickened. Taste and add more salt if needed.

Peas-and-Carrots Noodle Salad

5 ounces cellophane noodles (4 bundles)

4 ounces fresh sugar snap peas

3 tablespoons teriyaki sauce

1 tablespoon rice-wine vinegar

1 tablespoon grated fresh gingerroot

1 teaspoon dark sesame oil

pinch of sugar or to taste

pinch of salt or to taste

1/2 (10-ounce) bag julienned or shredded carrots
   (about 1 cup)

• Place noodles in bowl. Heat 1 quart water to boiling in 2-quart saucepan. Add snow peas; cook 2 minutes. Drain peas through strainer placed over bowl with noodles. Rinse peas with cold water to set color; pat dry. Soak noodles in the hot water until softened, 10 minutes.

• Mix teriyaki sauce, vinegar, ginger, oil, sugar, and salt in cup.

• Drain noodles well; place on serving plate. Snip with kitchen shears into 5-inch lengths. Top with sugar snaps and carrots. Drizzle dressing on top and toss to mix.

Fireside High Tea

• Welsh Griddle Cakes • Toasted Cheese
• Walnut-Curry Spread or Dip

MAKES 4 SERVINGS

"High" implies that a more substantial meal than just a snack will be served with the body-warming tea. It's an especially comforting occasion when it's cold outside.

GAME PLAN

1. Preheat broiler. Make curry spread or dip.
2. Toast bread; make cheese topping.
3. Make griddle cakes; toast cheese.

Welsh Griddle Cakes

These little pancakes were traditionally cooked on a cast-iron griddle or "girdle" hung over an open fire.

2 cups all-purpose flour

4 tablespoons unsalted butter

1/4 cup vegetable shortening

1/3 cup dried currants

1/3 cup plus 1 tablespoon sugar

1/2 teaspoon baking powder

1/2 teaspoon pumpkin pie spice mix, apple pie spice mix, or 1/4 teaspoon each ground cloves, ginger, cinnamon, and allspice

pinch of salt

2/3 cup milk plus more if needed

1 egg

• Place flour, butter, and shortening in a bowl; using pastry blender or 2 knives, cut through mixture until it resembles coarse crumbs. Add currants, sugar, baking powder, spice, and salt; mix. Make a well in the center. Mix milk and egg with a fork; pour into the well. Stir until mixed (dough will be stiff).

• Preheat griddle over medium-low heat. Roll out dough on lightly floured surface to 1/2- to 1/4-inch thickness. Cut into 21/2-inch rounds using a cookie cutter. Cook cakes on hot griddle until browned, about 3 minutes on each side. Serve immediately.

Makes 12 cakes.

Toasted Cheese

In the olden days the bread would be put on a long-handled fork and then toasted over an open fire. Then the cheese would be toasted (on the fork) until hot but not soft enough to fall off the fork (try that when you have time!) and then put on the toast.

4 thin slices good firm bread

2 tablespoons unsalted butter

2 tablespoons milk

1 cup grated or crumbled Caerphilly, Leicester, Cheshire, or cheddar cheese

2 to 3 teaspoons anchovy paste or to taste

• Preheat broiler. Line a baking sheet with foil. Place bread on top.

• Place butter and milk in medium microwave-safe bowl. Cover with microwave-safe plastic wrap; heat on high power until butter melts, 30 seconds. Add cheese; stir until blended.

• Broil bread on both sides 4 inches from heat source until crisp. Spread anchovy paste on 1 side of each slice; cover with cheese mixture. Broil until bubbling and lightly browned.

Walnut-Curry Spread or Dip

Here is a recipe that can go either way—if you want a spread use 1/4 cup yogurt and no more; for an instant dip just add 2 to 4 tablespoons more yogurt—whatever your pleasure.

1 (8-ounce) container whipped cream cheese with chives

1/4 cup chopped mango chutney

1 tablespoon mild curry powder

1/4 teaspoon cayenne pepper

fresh lemon juice to taste

1/4 cup plain yogurt (for spreading consistency; 2 to 4 tablespoons more for dipping consistency)

1/2 cup finely chopped freshly toasted walnuts

to use as a spread: whole-grain breads and crackers; British sweet meal biscuits; toasted raisin bread

to use as a dip: peeled baby carrots; Belgian endive leaves; peach, apple, and pear slices (cut immediately before serving or toss with lemon juice to keep from browning); toasted raisin bread, cut in squares or triangles

• Whisk cream cheese, chutney, curry, cayenne, and lemon juice in a medium bowl until blended. Whisk in yogurt for desired consistency. Spread in shallow serving bowl. Sprinkle with walnuts. Serve with breads for spreading or vegetables and fruits for dipping.

Makes about 2 cups.

Real Comfort Food Dinner

• Fried Cheesy Puffs • Ham Steaks with Apple-Rhubarb Sauce • Pumpkin-Yogurt Pudding

MAKES 4 SERVINGS

Sweet and salty ham goes with just about everything. Here's a mixture of some of its best flavor buddies.

GAME PLAN

1. Assemble pudding; refrigerate.
2. Fry ham and make sauce; keep warm.
3. Make and fry puffs.

Fried Cheesy Puffs

vegetable oil for frying

2 egg whites

2/3 cup grated Parmigiano-Reggiano or Pecorino-Romano cheese

1/2 teaspoon freshly ground pepper

• Heat 2 inches of oil to 375° in a wide sauté pan or saucepan. Meanwhile, whisk egg whites in large bowl until foamy and evenly broken up. Whisk in cheese and pepper. When oil is hot, fry teaspoonfuls of cheese mixture until puffed and brown, about 2 minutes. Drain on paper towels and serve immediately.

Ham Steaks with Apple-Rhubarb Sauce

1 tablespoon unsalted butter

1 tablespoon vegetable oil

1 (1¹/2-pound) trimmed boneless ham steak or 4 (6- to 8-ounce) boneless smoked pork chops

4 green onions, trimmed, cut crosswise into 1/4-inch-thick rounds

2 cups ³/4-inch pieces peeled rhubarb

1/2 cup sweet red vermouth

1 (4-ounce) container spiced applesauce (1/2 cup)

crème de cassis (black-currant liqueur) or sugar to taste

● Melt butter in oil in large nonstick skillet over high heat. Add ham and cook until browned, 1 to 2 minutes on each side. Remove to platter; cover with foil and keep warm.

● Reduce heat to medium-high; add onions to pan and sauté in drippings 3 minutes. Add rhubarb and vermouth; simmer until rhubarb is tender, about 4 minutes. Stir in applesauce. Sweeten to taste with liqueur or sugar. Serve sauce with ham.

Pumpkin-Yogurt Pudding

2 cups vanilla yogurt

1 cup pumpkin purée

1 teaspoon pumpkin pie spice

aerosol whipped-cream topping or sweetened whipped cream

ground cinnamon for dusting

● Combine yogurt, pumpkin, and pumpkin pie spice in bowl; mix well. Spoon into dessert dishes. Refrigerate for 10 minutes or until ready to serve. Garnish with topping and dust with cinnamon.

Fried Chicken with Japanese Flavors

• Crispy Chicken Thighs with Japanese Chili Seasoning
• Asian Lime Dipping Sauce • Cucumbers with Sweet Onion and
Soy Vinaigrette • Orange Berry Sundaes

MAKES 4 SERVINGS

The crunch of crispy fried chicken being eaten makes this is a meal for the senses. (You can make the chicken up to 1 hour in advance: Keep it warm in a 300° oven and cut into pieces just before serving.)

GAME PLAN
1. Flour chicken and begin to fry.
2. Make sundae sauce and salad. Turn chicken.
3. Make dipping sauce. Drain and slice chicken.

Crispy Chicken Thighs with Japanese Chili Seasoning

4 boneless chicken thighs (skin on)
vegetable oil for frying
1/2 cup rice flour
1 teaspoon Japanese chili seasoning (nanami togarashi) or Maryland-style seafood seasoning
1/2 teaspoon salt
Asian Lime Dipping Sauce (recipe follows)
lemon wedges for serving

• Rinse chicken with cold water; pat dry with paper towels. In a deep large skillet, heat 1/2 inch oil to shimmering over medium-high heat.

• Mix flour, chili seasoning, and salt in plastic food storage bag; add thighs one at a time and shake to coat. Fry chicken, turning after 5 minutes, until cooked through and crispy and golden on both sides, 10 to 15 minutes.

• Drain chicken on paper towels; cut crosswise into 1-inch slices (a Chinese cleaver is efficient for whacking and transferring the slices). Serve immediately with dipping sauce and lemon wedges.

Asian Lime Dipping Sauce

1/3 cup bottled sweetened lime juice, or 1/4 cup fresh
lime juice plus 2 tablespoons honey
1/4 cup Vietnamese or Thai fish sauce (nuoc mam or
nam pla) or low-sodium soy sauce
1/4 cup water
2 green onions, trimmed, thinly sliced
1 teaspoon Chinese garlic-chili sauce or sambal
oelek (Indonesian chili sauce; store-bought or see
recipe page 214) or to taste

• Mix ingredients in small bowl. This sauce is best used freshly made.

Cucumbers with Sweet Onion and Soy Vinaigrette

2 Kirby cucumbers, unpeeled, ends trimmed
1/4 cup finely chopped sweet onion such as Vidalia,
Maui, Texas Sweet, or Walla Walla
1/4 cup rice-wine vinegar
1 tablespoon low-sodium soy sauce
pinch of sugar

• Quarter cucumbers lengthwise; cut crosswise into 1/2-inch pieces. In a large bowl, combine cucumbers and remaining ingredients; toss.

Orange Berry Sundaes

If you think this is great on ice cream, try it with game, duck, and pork.

1 (11-ounce) can mandarin oranges, drained, juice
reserved
2 teaspoons cornstarch
1/2 cup walnut ice-cream topping
1 cup fresh wild or cultivated blueberries
fresh lemon juice to taste
vanilla ice cream

• Combine juice from oranges and cornstarch in small saucepan and blend. Add topping, heat to a boil and stir over medium-high heat. Boil 1 minute. Add oranges and berries. Season with lemon juice. Spoon sauce over ice cream and serve.

Feast from the Field, Forest, and Orchard

• Venison Steaks with Mushroom Juniper Sauce • Celeriac Sauté • Bourbon-Glazed Peaches

MAKES 4 SERVINGS

This is a menu for adventurous eaters, and one which will surprise those squeamish about trying new foods. Remember this when eating venison: Both farm-raised and wild meat share the virtue of delicious flavor and tenderness without growth hormones or steroids.

GAME PLAN

1. Thaw peaches. Start juniper sauce.
2. Sauté celeriac. Toss peaches with syrup.
3. Sauté mushrooms and then steaks.

Venison Steaks with Mushroom Juniper Sauce

2 tablespoons red currant jelly or grape jelly

2 cups hot water

1/2 (1-ounce) package French onion soup mix

3 juniper berries, finely crushed

2 tablespoons white-wine vinegar

1/2 teaspoon dried thyme leaves

2 tablespoons unsalted butter

12 ounces sliced mushrooms (cultivated, wild, or a mix)

1/4 teaspoon garlic powder or 2 garlic cloves, crushed

freshly ground pepper to taste

4 (1-inch-thick) venison steaks, trimmed, patted dry

• Make sauce: Whisk jelly with a little of the hot water in a 2-quart saucepan over medium-high heat until jelly melts. Add remaining water, soup mix, berries, vinegar, and thyme. Heat to boiling. Simmer, stirring occasionally, 10 minutes.

• Melt butter in large nonstick skillet over medium-high heat. Add mushrooms and garlic powder and sauté until tender, 2 minutes. When juniper sauce has simmered 10 minutes, stir in mushrooms. Taste for seasoning and add pepper if needed. Keep sauce warm.

• Season steaks with pepper. In unwashed skillet used to cook mushrooms, sauté steaks over medium-high heat until browned, 1 to 1 1/2 minutes per side. Remove to warm plates. Serve sauce with steaks.

Celeriac Sauté

1 (24-ounce) jar julienned celeriac (about 2 cups drained)
2 tablespoons unsalted butter
salt and freshly ground pepper to taste
dried marjoram to taste

● Drain celeriac in a colander and rinse.

● Melt butter in large skillet over medium-high heat; add celeriac and sauté until lightly browned, 5 to 7 minutes. Season with salt, pepper, and marjoram to taste.

Bourbon-Glazed Peaches

1 (16- to 20-ounce) bag frozen sliced peaches
4 tablespoons unsalted butter
1/4 cup brown sugar
1/4 cup bourbon
1/4 teaspoon ground cinnamon

● Thaw peaches in bowl in microwave as package label directs.

● Combine remaining ingredients in small saucepan over medium heat. Stir until butter and sugar melt and syrup boils. Add to peaches; stir to coat.

Why Just Dream of Dining in Marseilles?

• Quick Bouillabaisse • Harissa-Spiked Rouille • Iced Grapes in Pastis

MAKES 4 SERVINGS

Put on your beret and the songs of Edith Piaf; you can be on the Mediterranean in your heart, mind, and palate with this very easy version of the usually intimidating classic French soup.

GAME PLAN

1. Start saffron broth for bouillabaisse.
2. Pulse, drizzle, and freeze grapes.
3. Make rouille. Add fish to soup.

Quick Bouillabaisse

1 tablespoon olive oil

1 bulb fennel, stems discarded, chopped (reserve fern)

1/2 teaspoon saffron threads

2 cups chicken broth or fish stock

1 (16-ounce) can stewed tomatoes

grated zest and juice of 1 orange

1 teaspoon dried thyme

8 ounces thick fish fillets, cut into 1/2-inch pieces

4 shelled, deveined medium shrimp

1 pound mussels, scrubbed

salt and freshly ground pepper to taste

croutons

Harissa-Spiked Rouille (recipe follows)

• Heat oil in 3-quart saucepan over medium-high heat. Add fennel and sauté 2 minutes. Add saffron and broth and heat to boiling. Add tomatoes, orange zest, thyme, and orange juice. Reduce heat to medium-low and simmer 10 minutes, stirring occasionally.

• Increase heat to medium-high. When mixture boils, add fish and shellfish; cover and cook 2 minutes, until mussels open and shrimp are pink. Remove from heat. Taste and adjust seasonings. Add a few croutons to each bowl; ladle soup on top. Serve with rouille.

Harissa-Spiked Rouille

The North African influence on French cuisine shows that sometimes it's right to shake up the establishment a little. This recipe celebrates flavors and spices so enticing, they have to cross cultural boundaries.

1 (7-ounce) jar roasted red peppers
1 egg yolk
2 tablespoons red-wine vinegar
1 teaspoon harissa (Tunisian pepper sauce; store-bought or see recipe page 214) or more to taste
1/4 teaspoon garlic salt or 2 garlic cloves, crushed through a press
1/2 cup olive oil
juice of 1/2 lemon or more to taste

● Combine peppers, egg yolk, vinegar, harissa, and garlic salt in food processor; purée. With machine running, pour in oil in a slow, steady stream until emulsified. Season with lemon juice and more harissa.

Makes 4 to 6 servings.

Iced Grapes in Pastis

4 cups mixed seedless green, red, and black grapes
1/2 cup pastis or other licorice-flavored aperitif or liqueur
1 tablespoon orange-flower water
mint sprigs for garnish

● Pulse grapes in food processor until coarsely chopped. Pour into a bowl and drizzle with pastis and orange-flower water. Toss to mix. Place in goblets and freeze 15 minutes. Garnish with mint.

Early Dinner on the Deck

• Pimiento Cheese with Chips and Crudités • Brunswick Stew • Blackberry and Dulce de Leche Gratin

MAKES 4 SERVINGS

When the days seem endless and the sun takes a long time to set, dining al fresco is required. Have the torches, mosquito coils, and citronella candles ready to light, and watch the stars come out as you eat.

GAME PLAN

1. Make stew. Preheat broiler.
2. Make pimiento cheese.
3. Assemble gratin and broil.

Pimiento Cheese with Chips and Crudités

This is a staple food in the American South, where you can find it already made in the refrigerator case. It makes squishy white bread taste like gold and is as delicious licked off your fingertip as it is from the curl of a crisp salty corn chip or a cold juicy celery stalk.

1 cup (4 ounces) shredded Cheddar cheese
1 (2-ounce) jar chopped pimientos, drained
2 green onions, trimmed, finely chopped
2 to 4 tablespoons regular or bacon-flavored
  mayonnaise

pinch of Maryland-style seafood seasoning
corn chips and crudités (cut up vegetables such as
  carrots, celery, bell pepper) for dipping

• Mix cheese, pimientos, onions, mayonnaise, and seasoning together to an easily spreadable consistency. Serve with chips and vegetables.

BUY TIME

If you don't want to roast the corn, just use canned or frozen corn.

Brunswick Stew

This early American Southern specialty was made with squirrel and simmered for hours in cast-iron cauldrons over wood fires under the trees. This quick version has all the flavor of yesteryear but is made with chicken.

1 (14.5-ounce) can diced tomatoes with mild chilies
1/2 cup dry white wine
4 (4-ounce) boneless, skinless chicken breasts
1 (10-ounce) package frozen baby lima beans
1 (10-ounce) package frozen cut okra (optional)
2 ears corn on the cob, shucked
1 teaspoon Worcestershire sauce
Tabasco sauce to taste
freshly ground pepper to taste

• Heat tomatoes with their juices and wine in a 2-quart saucepan to simmering over medium-high heat. Add chicken, covering with a round of parchment the diameter of the pan and lid. Reduce heat to medium; poach chicken until cooked through, about 15 minutes.

• Meanwhile, cook limas and okra in microwave as package labels direct. Roast corn by placing ears directly on a gas burner or broil on a broiler rack 3 inches from the heat source. Turn until charred on all sides, 3 to 4 minutes in all. Remove with tongs to cutting board. Cut off kernels, scraping cobs to extract milky juice.

• Remove chicken from tomatoes; place on warm plates. Stir corn, limas, and okra and their cooking juices, Worcestershire sauce, and Tabasco into tomatoes. Heat through. Season liberally with pepper; spoon on top of the chicken.

Blackberry and Dulce de Leche Gratin

unsalted butter for greasing pan plus 2 tablespoons for gratin
4 cups fresh blackberries
2 eggs
2/3 cup canned dulce de leche or sweetened condensed milk
1/3 cup milk
1/4 teaspoon ground cinnamon
1/4 cup gingersnap, graham-cracker, or other cookie crumbs
lime sherbet (optional)

• Preheat broiler. Grease a 10-inch gratin dish or a 1 1/2-quart baking dish with butter. Spread out berries in prepared dish.

• Whisk eggs, dulce de leche, milk, and cinnamon in bowl until blended; pour over berries. Sprinkle with crumbs and dot with remaining butter. Broil 6 inches from heat source until crumbs are browned and custard is bubbly, about 5 minutes. Let cool before serving. Serve with scoops of sherbet alongside.

BUY TIME

Have all the flavors of this dish without cooking by serving fresh blackberries over scoops of dulce de leche ice cream.

Jazz Concert Picnic Under the Stars

• Quick Chopped Liver • Cold Avocado Soup
• Smoked Pork with Basil and Tomatoes

MAKES 4 SERVINGS

This menu works to host a foursome enjoying the music or as a contribution to a larger party sharing a potluck spread. The pork is served room temperature in the salad.

GAME PLAN
1. Preheat broiler; cook pork.
2. Make chopped liver. Make soup.
3. Assemble salad.

Quick Chopped Liver

1 chicken bouillon cube
2 cups boiling water
1/2 pound chicken livers, trimmed, rinsed, and
  patted dry
1/2 cup deli egg salad or more if needed
2 slender green onions, trimmed, minced
salt and freshly ground pepper to taste
Melba toast and crudités (cut up vegetables such as
  carrots, celery, and bell peppers)

• Make chicken broth from bouillon and boiling water in a small saucepan. Add livers and simmer, covered, until cooked through and barely pink in centers, 6 to 8 minutes. Drain, reserving liquid.

• Process livers in food processor until mixed but with some interesting texture, adding enough cooking liquid to moisten livers so that they chop easily. Scrape mixture into a bowl. Add 1/2 cup egg salad, onions, salt, and pepper. Add more egg salad if mixture needs it for flavor or texture. Serve with Melba toast and crudités.

Makes about 1 1/2 cups.

Smoked Pork with Basil and Tomatoes

Use a mixture of sliced ripe heirloom tomatoes instead of plum tomatoes to take advantage of the late summer tomato boom.

3 tablespoons balsamic vinaigrette (store-bought
    or see recipe page 215)
3 tablespoons sun-dried tomato pesto (store-bought
    or see recipe page 213)
4 (5-ounce) boneless smoked pork chops
2 red plum tomatoes
2 yellow plum tomatoes
2 tablespoons fresh lemon juice
1 Kirby cucumber, diced
2 cups fresh basil leaves
1 roasted red pepper (store-bought or homemade),
    sliced
2 cups herb or garlic croutons (store-bought or
    homemade)

• Preheat broiler. Line small shallow broiler pan with foil. Mix vinaigrette and pesto in a large bowl; spread half of mixture on both sides of pork. Place pork in prepared pan and broil 4 inches from heat source, until sizzling and browned, 2 to 3 minutes on each side. Set aside to cool.

PICNIC NOTE

If you are taking this on a picnic, toss everything except the croutons in the serving container. Pack the croutons in a plastic food storage bag; add just before serving.

• Halve tomatoes lengthwise; using your thumb, scoop out and discard seeds. Sliver tomatoes. Stir lemon juice into remaining vinaigrette mixture. Add tomatoes, cucumber, basil, and red pepper and toss to mix.

• Slice pork into 1/2-inch-wide strips; add to vegetables. Add croutons and toss.

Cold Avocado Soup

2 ripe avocados, pitted, peeled
juice of 1 lime or more to taste
2 cups plain yogurt
2 cups milk
4 fresh basil leaves, torn
pinch of cayenne pepper
salt and freshly ground pepper to taste

• Cut avocados into large chunks; place in food processor with lime juice and yogurt. Pulse until blended; process until smooth. Scrape into a 2-quart bowl or plastic food storage container; whisk in milk. Stir in basil. Season with cayenne, salt, and pepper. Cover; refrigerate until serving.

So Many Flavors in So Little Time

• Corn Soup with Chipotle Cream • Warm Shrimp Salad Wraps • Portuguese Sugared Oranges

MAKES 4 SERVINGS

With lip-warming chilies, tortillas in a warm embrace, and sugar-coated oranges bursting with juice, this is not a meal to rush through.

GAME PLAN

1. Start soup. Make chipotle cream.
2. Cook shrimp.
3. Prepare oranges. Heat tortillas and assemble wraps.

Corn Soup with Chipotle Cream

2 slices bacon, chopped

1 leek, trimmed, cut into rings, rinsed well

1 (1-pound) bag frozen corn kernels

2 cups vegetable or chicken broth

2 cups heavy cream

1 tablespoon sundried-tomato paste or regular tomato paste

2 teaspoons chipotles in adobo, chopped, or 1 teaspoon crushed dried chipotles

1/4 cup white wine or more if needed

1/2 cup crème fraîche

salt and freshly ground pepper to taste

• Cook bacon and leeks in 3-quart saucepan over medium-high heat until leeks are tender and color slightly, about 3 minutes. Add corn, broth, and cream and heat to boiling. Simmer 5 to 10 minutes.

• Meanwhile, cook tomato paste and chipotles in a small nonstick skillet over medium heat until sizzling. Remove from heat and whisk in wine until blended. Whisk in crème fraîche and more wine if needed to make mixture pourable.

• Taste soup and season with salt and pepper. Spoon soup into bowls and drizzle with chipotle cream.

Warm Shrimp Salad Wraps

1/4 cup balsamic vinaigrette (store-bought or
  see recipe page 215)

1 pound shelled, deveined small shrimp

1/2 small bulb fennel, thinly sliced

1/2 red onion, thinly sliced

1/2 teaspoon dill weed

1/4 teaspoon garlic powder

salt and freshly ground pepper to taste

8 (8-inch) red-pepper flavored flour tortillas

2 cups cleaned baby spinach

1 plum tomato, chopped

• Heat vinaigrette to boiling in large nonstick skillet over medium heat. Add shrimp, fennel, onion, dill, and garlic powder and mix well. Cover and cook until shrimp are cooked, curled, and pink, about 5 minutes. Remove from heat. Stir, taste, and season with salt and pepper.

• Warm tortillas as package label directs. Arrange spinach down center of each tortilla; sprinkle with tomato. Top with shrimp mixture and roll up. Place seam side down on serving dishes.

Portuguese Sugared Oranges

4 navel oranges

4 teaspoons sugar

• Cut oranges crosswise in half, if you'd like. Cut away the peel from the top 1/2 inch of cut side of each half. Sprinkle the cut side of fruit with sugar. Serve with grapefruit spoons.

Happy Italian Family Meal

• Garlic Scallop and Shrimp Dunk • *Italian Bread*
• *A Big Green Salad with Red-Wine Vinaigrette*
• Gnocchi with Gorgonzola Sauce • Mascarpone Tiramisù

MAKES 4 SERVINGS

There is something about this meal that makes for a warm feeling around the table. Everyone feels like part of the family—even if it's just friends!

GAME PLAN

1. Heat water for gnocchi. Preheat broiler. Assemble tiramisù and refrigerate.
2. Prepare tomato sauce. Cook gnocchi and make gorgonzola sauce.
3. Cook seafood. Coat gnocchi with sauce and broil.

Garlic Scallop and Shrimp Dunk

Serve with slices of crusty Italian bread for sopping up the tasty sauce. Or you can stretch this to feed extra guests by tossing it with a pound of cooked pasta.

1/4 cup extra-virgin olive oil

1 head garlic, sliced horizontally in half, loose outside skin removed

2 cups of 1/2-inch diced red, yellow, orange, and green bell peppers

2 (14 1/2-ounce) cans stewed tomatoes

1 teaspoon dried oregano

1 teaspoon dried basil

freshly ground pepper and salt to taste

1 pound scallops, muscles removed

1 pound peeled, deveined shrimp

8 leaves fresh basil, torn or shredded

• Combine oil and garlic head halves, cut sides down, in a deep medium skillet. Cook over medium heat until garlic is golden and aromatic, about 2 minutes.

• Add bell peppers; sauté 1 minute. Add tomatoes and mash with a potato masher; stir in dried herbs and season with pepper. Cook over medium-high heat, stirring occasionally, 10 minutes. Remove garlic.

• Stir in scallops and shrimp; simmer just until scallops are opaque and shrimp are pink and curled, about 3 minutes. Taste and adjust seasoning if needed. Sprinkle with fresh basil.

Gnocchi with Gorgonzola Sauce

nonstick cooking spray
1 (1-pound) package shelf-stable gnocchi (potato, spinach, or tomato)
4 ounces Gorgonzola cheese, crumbled
4 tablespoons unsalted butter, cut into pieces
1 cup light cream or half-and-half
1/4 teaspoon cracked pepper
1/2 cup chopped walnuts

• Heat 2 quarts water in deep skillet to boiling. Preheat broiler. Grease 2-quart broiler-safe baking dish or gratin dish with cooking spray.

• Add gnocchi to boiling water and cook until they float, about 3 minutes. Remove to prepared baking dish with slotted spoon.

• Combine cheese, butter, cream, and pepper in small saucepan over medium heat. Cook, whisking occasionally, until smooth; pour over gnocchi. Sprinkle with nuts. Broil 6 inches from heat source until bubby, about 5 minutes.

Mascarpone Tiramisù

Cookie crumbs, ladyfingers, sponge cake, and cupcakes can all be used instead of pound cake.

1/2 cup strong coffee
2 tablespoons confectioners' sugar
2 tablespoons brandy
4 thick slices pound cake
1 cup mascarpone cheese or vanilla pudding
1/4 cup mini chocolate chips

• Mix coffee, sugar, and brandy in a small bowl; brush over cake slices and place in compotes or goblets. Mix mascarpone and chips; spoon over cake slices.

Fresh Fish from the Steamer

• Sake-Steamed Fish • Broccoli with Sake, Wasabi, and Ginger Butter • Soba Salad • *Assorted Sorbets with Crisp Cookies*

MAKES 4 SERVINGS

Japanese are masters with fish, raw and cooked, and with ingredients that make meals almost a religious experience. Offer green tea and chilled sake to drink.

GAME PLAN

1. Heat water for soba. Prepare steamer with baskets. Make wasabi butter and soba sauce.
2. Assemble fish in bowl in one steamer basket; place broccoli in another bowl in other basket.
3. Cook soba. Steam fish and broccoli. Toss soba with dressing. Toss broccoli with wasabi butter.

Sake-Steamed Fish

4 (6-ounce) skinless mild fish fillets (flounder, fluke, or rainbow trout)

1/2 teaspoon fine sea salt

2 tablespoons sake

1 tablespoon mirin (sweet rice wine)

2 teaspoons low-sodium soy sauce plus extra for serving

2 green onions, trimmed, finely chopped

2 tablespoons sliced pickled ginger or slivered peeled fresh gingerroot

• Prepare wok or wide steamer with boiling water. Gently rinse fish; pat dry. Fold thinner ends under fillets and place in a shallow bowl that will fit into a wok or steamer. Sprinkle fish with salt. Mix sake, mirin and soy sauce; pour over fish. Sprinkle with onions and ginger.

• Place bowl in wok or steamer rack over boiling water. Cover and steam until fish is cooked through, about 5 minutes. Carefully remove lid and serve immediately.

Broccoli with Sake, Wasabi and Ginger Butter

You can use prepared wasabi sauce (from a bottle or a tube) or grated fresh peeled wasabi instead of the powdered variety.

2 tablespoons powdered wasabi (Japanese horseradish)
2 tablespoons sake
2 tablespoons slivered pickled ginger, with juices
4 tablespoons unsalted butter, whisked until creamy
*   for easier blending*
2 cups broccoli florets

• Prepare wok or steamer with boiling water. Blend wasabi with sake in bowl; stir in ginger and juices. Stir in butter until blended. Pack into a ramekin and use immediately; or roll in butter wrapper into a 1-inch cylinder and chill or freeze.

• Place broccoli in shallow bowl. Place bowl in wok or steamer over boiling water. Cover and steam until broccoli is tender, about 5 minutes. In serving bowl, toss broccoli with wasabi butter to taste.

Soba Salad

You can serve this hot, warm, or chilled.

8 ounces soba (Japanese buckwheat noodles)
3 teaspoons dark sesame oil
4 green onions, trimmed, quartered lengthwise,
*   cut crosswise into 1-inch pieces*
1 red and 1 green bell pepper, seeded, cut into
*   1-inch strips*
2 tablespoons low-sodium soy sauce
2 tablespoons rice vinegar
2 teaspoons sugar

• Heat 2 quarts water in large deep skillet to boiling. Add noodles and return water to boiling. Add 1 cup cold water, return water to boiling and add 1/2 cup cold water. Boil again, add another 1/2 cup cold water and cook until al dente, 3 minutes (taste for doneness). Drain in strainer and rinse noodles with hot water. Place in medium bowl; toss with 1 teaspoon sesame oil. Add onions and peppers; toss.

• Mix remaining oil, soy sauce, vinegar, and sugar in small cup; pour over noodles. Toss.

Menu for "Falling in Love Again" over Veal Cutlets

• Guenther's Veal à la Holstein • Spaetzle with Caraway Butter • Sautéed Apple Rings

MAKES 4 SERVINGS

Marlene Dietrich would have loved this menu. It's simple and fun to prepare, and quite delicious.

GAME PLAN

1. Heat water for spaetzle. Preheat oven. Slice and fry apples.
2. Make spaetzle. Keep apples and spaetzle warm in oven.
3. Coat and fry cutlets; fry eggs.

Guenther's Veal à la Holstein

4 (6- to 8-ounce) veal cutlets, pounded lightly
   by butcher
salt and pepper to taste
5 eggs
4 tablespoons water
1/4 cup all-purpose flour
1/2 cup plain dried bread crumbs
5 tablespoons unsalted butter
2 tablespoons oil
8 anchovy fillets, rinsed

1/4 cup fresh lemon juice
1 tablespoon chopped fresh parsley
1 teaspoon capers, rinsed

• Preheat oven to 300°. Season the veal with salt and pepper. Mix 1 egg with 2 tablespoons water in shallow bowl. Place flour and bread crumbs in separate shallow bowls. Dredge veal in the flour, shake off excess. Dip into the egg wash, allow excess to drip off. Coat with the bread crumbs.

• Melt 2 tablespoons butter in the oil in a large skillet until very hot. (Sprinkle a few crumbs in the fat; it

150

It will take about 10 minutes for 2 quarts of water to come to boiling in a 14-inch deep skillet compared to 14 minutes in an 8-inch-wide, 3-quart saucepan. When you're in a hurry, you want to save every second!

should bubble immediately.) Cook veal on both sides until golden brown, about 4 minutes in all. Remove to an oven-safe platter, cover loosely with foil, and keep warm in oven.

• Drain off fat from pan; wipe out pan with paper towel. Melt 2 tablespoons butter over medium-high heat. Crack the remaining eggs into the skillet, season with salt and pepper and add the remaining water. Cover pan, reduce heat to medium, and cook eggs until perfect sunny side up (the yolks should be runny).

• Place a cooked egg on top of each cutlet, arrange 2 anchovy fillets in a cross over each yolk and keep warm. In the same pan, melt and brown the remaining butter, add lemon juice, parsley, and capers and pour the sauce over the eggs and cutlets.

Spaetzle with Caraway Butter

Are they noodles or dumplings? However this German comfort food should be categorized, it's a quick-to-make, quick-to-cook, delicious side dish. A spaetzle-maker only costs about 5 dollars—it's worth every penny.

salt
2 1/2 cups all-purpose flour
2 eggs
3/4 cup water or more if needed
4 tablespoons unsalted butter, softened, in pieces
1 to 2 teaspoons caraway seeds

• Heat 2 quarts lightly salted water in deep skillet. Meanwhile, mix flour and 1/2 teaspoon salt in bowl; make a well in center and add eggs. Whisk eggs with fork until broken; whisk in a little water at a time, quickly incorporating the flour. Stir until smooth, adding enough water to make the texture of a thick batter. (Do not overbeat.)

• Pass batter through a spaetzle maker or a colander held over the boiling water. Cook spaetzle until they rise to the surface, about 2 minutes. Remove as they cook with a slotted spoon into a strainer in a serving bowl. When all the spaetzle are retrieved, drain and return spaetzle to the bowl (the bowl will have been warmed with the water). Add butter and caraway; toss until butter melts. Serve immediately or cover and keep warm in a 300° oven until serving.

Note: Cooked buttered spaetzle freezes beautifully. Pack a batch in a plastic freezer-weight food storage bag and freeze it flat so that it will thaw quickly.

Sautéed Apple Rings

You can fry these before dinner; reheat if desired when you're ready for dessert.

2 Rome or Granny Smith apples

2 tablespoons cinnamon sugar or plain sugar
*   for sprinkling*

2 tablespoons unsalted butter plus extra for greasing
*   serving dish*

pinch of grated nutmeg

1/4 cup apple juice or white wine

Quark or crème fraîche for serving

● Core whole apples and slice crosswise into 1/2-inch-thick rings; sprinkle both sides with cinnamon sugar. Melt butter in nonstick skillet over medium-high heat. Add apples and nutmeg; sauté until caramelized, about 2 minutes on each side.

● Butter a serving dish or individual plates. Arrange apple slices in prepared dish. Add apple juice to hot skillet and heat to boiling, scraping up browned bits. Boil until reduced to 2 tablespoons; pour over apples. Serve warm or at room temperature with Quark.

Note: Quark is German-style crème fraîche/sour cream. It can be found in German food stores, but lovely Quark is also made by American cheese producers and sold in cheese shops and specialty food stores.

Mardi Gras Dinner Party

• Jambalaya Stir-Fry • Spicy Andouille Rice • Baked Rum-Buttered Bananas

MAKES 4 SERVINGS

No need to wait until early spring to have this festive meal! The flavors are bound to set you dancing any time of year.

GAME PLAN

1. Preheat oven and melt butter. Start rice.
2. Bake bananas.
3. Stir-fry jambalaya.

Jambalaya Stir-Fry

This traditional baked rice casserole is fun to deconstruct and serve in parts.

1 tablespoon vegetable oil
2 ribs celery, cut into 1/4-inch wide diagonal slices
1 large green bell pepper, seeded, thinly sliced
8 ounces smoked ham, cut into 1/2-inch strips
1 (5-ounce) skinless, boneless chicken breast half,
  cut into thin strips
1 (16-ounce) jar hot picante sauce
1 cup water

1 1/2 pounds peeled, deveined medium shrimp
salt and Tabasco sauce to taste, if needed
torn fresh Italian parsley for garnish

• Heat oil in a wok or large heavy skillet over high heat. Add celery and pepper and stir-fry 1 minute. Add ham and chicken; stir-fry 2 minutes. Add picante sauce and water; cover and heat to boiling.

• Add shrimp; remove pan from heat. Cover; let stand until shrimp are cooked, 5 minutes. Season with salt and Tabasco and sprinkle with parsley.

Spicy Andouille Rice

1 1/2 cups white rice

1/2 pound andouille sausage or kielbasa, cut into
    1/4-inch slices

3 cups water

1 bunch green onions, trimmed, chopped

● Rinse rice; place in 2-quart saucepan. Add sausage and water; heat to boiling over medium-high heat, partially covered. Reduce heat and simmer until rice is cooked, about 15 minutes. Add onions; toss with wooden salad fork. Cover; let stand 5 minutes.

Makes 4 to 6 servings.

Baked Rum-Buttered Bananas

This oven-baked rendition of Bananas Foster works well when you're busy with other pots on the stove.

2 tablespoons unsalted butter

1/4 cup bottled sweetened lime juice

1/4 cup dark rum

1/2 teaspoon ground allspice

4 medium bananas, not too soft, peeled, halved
    crosswise and lengthwise

vanilla frozen yogurt

● Preheat oven to 350°. Place butter in 9-inch square baking pan or dish; set it in the oven to melt as the oven heats up.

● Remove pan; stir in lime juice, rum, and allspice. Add bananas; turn to coat. Bake 12 minutes, turning and basting with pan juices after 6 minutes.

● Cover with foil; keep warm until serving. (You can turn off the oven and let them stay there.) Serve with frozen yogurt.

Take Me to the Casbah!

• Moroccan Chicken • Couscous with Olives, Preserved Lemon, and Dates • Poached Apricots with Pistachios and Chèvre

MAKES 4 SERVINGS

Pull out your video of *Casablanca* and invite your best friends in for an exotic culinary escape.

GAME PLAN
1. Prepare chicken; start to cook.
2. Heat water for couscous. Poach apricots.
3. Cook couscous.

Moroccan Chicken

There's a bit of measuring for the spice mix but after the chicken starts to cook you can get on to other things.

4 boneless chicken thighs (skin on)
2 garlic cloves, crushed through a press
2 tablespoons olive oil
1 teaspoon kosher salt
1 teaspoon ground cumin
1 teaspoon ground ginger
1/2 teaspoon paprika (preferably Spanish)
1/2 teaspoon ground cinnamon
1/2 teaspoon ground turmeric
1/4 teaspoon freshly ground pepper
2 tablespoons vegetable oil

• Rinse chicken with cold water; pat dry with paper towels. Mix garlic, olive oil, salt, and spices; rub over chicken.

• Heat vegetable oil to shimmering over medium-high heat. Add chicken; cook, partially covered, turning after 5 minutes, until cooked through and crispy on both sides, 10 to 15 minutes. Let stand 5 minutes; cut crosswise into 1-inch slices.

156

Couscous with Olives, Preserved Lemon, and Dates

The flavors of Northern Africa are at hand in most grocery stores if you have the initiative to look. If you can't find preserved lemons, just make some!

1 3/4 cups water
1 1/2 cups couscous
1 cup imported olives (preferably spicy Moroccan or
   Tunisian mix), pitted, marinating juices reserved
8 plump pitted dates, quartered lengthwise
rind of 1 preserved lemon (store-bought, or see recipe
   page 218), slivered

• Bring the water to boiling in small saucepan; add couscous, olives and their juices, dates, and lemon rind. Stir, cover, and remove from heat. Fluff with fork. Let stand at least 5 minutes.

Poached Apricots with Pistachios and Chèvre

16 dried apricots
1 cup orange juice
3 cardamom pods, crushed, hulls discarded
4 ounces young chèvre (goat's milk cheese)
1/4 cup chopped unsalted shelled pistachios

• Combine apricots, orange juice, and cardamom seeds in a small saucepan; cover and heat to simmering over medium heat. Cook until apricots are puffed but not split, about 5 minutes. Remove from heat. Set aside, covered, until ready to serve.

• Spoon apricots into bowls; add a dollop of cheese and sprinkle with nuts.

Easy Antipasto Dinner Party

• Antipasto Buffet Platter • Black Bean and Butternut Squash Bruschetta • Broiled Fig and Prosciutto Bruschetta • Grilled Summer Squash Bruschetta • Sliced Raw Mushrooms with Lemon • Marinated Chickpeas

MAKES 4 SERVINGS

There's enough food here to feed Caesar's army, and it can be pulled together before you can say, "by Jove!" The bruschetta toasts can be made together and you just have to top them assembly-line fashion.

GAME PLAN

1. Preheat broiler. Assemble buffet platter. Make ham roses.
2. Mix chickpeas. Season mushrooms. Sauté bean topping.
3. Broil figs and summer squash and then breads. Assemble bruschetta.

Antipasto Buffet Platter

inner leaves from a head of Romaine lettuce
1 (8-ounce) wedge Gorgonzola cheese
1 (8-ounce) wedge Parmigiano-Reggiano cheese
8 ounces small marinated mozzarella cheese balls
1 (9-ounce) jar pepperoncini, drained
1 (7-ounce) jar roasted red peppers, drained, cut into strips
1 (6-ounce) jar marinated artichoke hearts, drained
1/2 cup mixed olives
1 bulb fresh fennel, trimmed, cut into thin wedges
cold celery hearts, ribs separated

8 ounces thinly sliced Genoa salami
4 ounces thinly sliced mortadella, folded into loose cones
Italian breadsticks
Italian fennel bread rings (Taralli con Finocchietto)

• Arrange lettuce on large platter or cutting board. Surround with cheeses. Fill lettuce with pepperoncini, peppers, artichoke hearts, and olives. Fill in gaps on platter with fennel, celery, salami, and mortadella. Place breadsticks in heavy-bottomed glass; place bread rings in basket.

Makes 6 to 8 servings.

Black Bean and Butternut Squash Bruschetta

1 tablespoon unsalted butter

1 tablespoon extra-virgin olive oil plus extra for
  brushing

1 cup finely diced peeled butternut squash

1/2 teaspoon garlic salt

2 tablespoons water

1 cup rinsed canned black beans

2 marinated sun-dried tomatoes, slivered, plus
  1 tablespoon oil from tomatoes

salt to taste

4 (3/4-inch-thick) slices crusty firm country-style
  Italian bread

dried oregano and freshly ground black pepper
  to taste

• Preheat broiler. Melt butter in oil in medium skillet. Add squash and sprinkle with garlic salt; sauté 2 minutes. Add water, beans, and tomatoes with marinating oil; cover and cook until squash is tender, 3 minutes. Continue to cook, crushing some of the squash and beans to a paste and adding a little water if needed to keep squash from sticking, 2 minutes. Taste and adjust salt if needed.

• Place bread on baking sheet; broil 4 inches from heat source until toasted on both sides. Spread bean mixture on one side of each toast. Sprinkle with oregano and pepper.

Broiled Fig and Prosciutto Bruschetta

olive oil for brushing and drizzling

8 black Mission figs, thinly sliced

fine brown sugar

4 (3/4-inch-thick) slices crusty firm country-style
  Italian bread

4 slices (thicker than paper-thin) prosciutto di Parma

• Preheat broiler. Line broiler pan with foil; grease foil with oil. Arrange figs on foil, sprinkle with sugar, and broil 4 inches from heat source until caramelized. Place bread on baking sheet; broil 4 inches from heat source until toasted on both sides. Drizzle toast on one side with oil. Top with prosciutto and figs.

Grilled Summer Squash Bruschetta

1 small zucchini, thinly sliced

1 small yellow summer squash, thinly sliced

Caesar salad dressing or citrus vinaigrette (store-
  bought or see recipes pages 216 and 217) for
  brushing

4 (3/4-inch-thick) slices crusty firm country-style
  Italian bread

8 to 12 leaves cleaned arugula

shavings of Parmigiano-Reggiano cheese for serving

fresh oregano sprigs for serving

● Preheat broiler. Line baking sheet with foil; arrange zucchini and squash slices in a single layer on foil and brush with dressing. Broil 4 inches from heat source, turning after 4 to 5 minutes and brushing with dressing after turning, until golden brown, 8 to 10 minutes. Place bread on baking sheet; broil 4 inches from heat source until toasted on both sides.

● Arrange arugula on toasts; brush with dressing. Top with alternating slices of both kinds of squash, the cheese, and then sprigs of oregano.

Sliced Raw Mushrooms with Lemon

8 ounces sliced small white mushrooms (buy them
* already sliced)*
finely shredded zest and juice of 1 lemon
extra-virgin olive oil for drizzling
kosher salt and freshly ground black pepper to taste
wedge of Parmigiano-Reggiano cheese

● Spread out mushrooms on a flat plate. Drizzle with lemon juice and oil. Sprinkle with lemon zest, salt, and pepper. Shred curls of Parmigiano-Reggiano on top.

Marinated Chickpeas

1 (10 1/2-ounce) can chickpeas, drained, rinsed
2 tablespoons Caesar salad dressing (store-bought or
* see recipe page 217)*
2 tablespoons chopped fresh parsley
squeeze of fresh lemon juice, plus lemon wedges for
* serving*
dried oregano and freshly ground pepper to taste
1 crisp inner radicchio leaf

● Combine chickpeas, dressing, parsley, lemon juice, oregano, and pepper in a bowl; toss to mix. Arrange radicchio "bowl" on a serving dish; fill with chickpeas. Serve with lemon wedges.

Sunday Dinner for Company

• Peach Bellinis • Grilled Mustard-Dill Salmon
• Linguine with Asparagus and Lemon Cream Sauce
• Candied Apricots and Sweet Cheese Bites

MAKES 4 SERVINGS

Welcome friends or visitors passing through with this meal that's special but not a big production number.

GAME PLAN

1. Heat water for pasta. Prepare grill or preheat broiler.
2. Make pasta sauce. Prepare fish. Assemble cheese bites. Prepare Bellinis.
3. Cook pasta and asparagus; toss with sauce. Broil fish.

Peach Bellinis

1 cup peach nectar
1 (25-ounce) bottle chilled sparkling wine

• Pour 1/4 cup peach nectar into 4 champagne flutes; top with sparkling wine.

Grilled Mustard-Dill Salmon

nonstick cooking spray
2 tablespoons honey mustard
4 (6-ounce) skinless salmon fillets, 3/4-inch-thick
1 teaspoon dried dillweed
1/2 teaspoon lemon-pepper seasoning
2 teaspoons olive oil

• Prepare charcoal or gas grill and heat to high, or preheat broiler. (If using broiler, line broiler pan with foil; grease foil with cooking spray and add fillets.)

- Spread mustard over boned side of fillets; sprinkle with dill and pepper seasoning. Drizzle with oil.

- Grill or broil salmon 4 to 5 inches from heat source until desired doneness, 6 to 8 minutes. Let stand off heat, loosely covered with foil, 5 minutes before serving.

Linguine with Asparagus and Lemon Cream Sauce

For an extra treat, add 1 cup diced tomato to the lemon cream sauce.

salt
1 large lemon
1 cup heavy cream
8 fresh basil leaves, shredded
1/2 teaspoon lemon pepper
1 pound thin asparagus, trimmed, cut into 1-inch pieces
8 ounces linguine

- Heat 2 quarts salted water to boiling in large deep skillet.

- Remove 2 tablespoons grated zest and then 3 table-spoons juice from lemon; place in another large deep skillet. Add cream, basil, 3/4 teaspoon salt, and the lemon pepper. Heat to boiling; reduce heat to medium-low and simmer.

- Cook asparagus in the boiling water until desired doneness, 2 to 3 minutes. Remove to sauce with slotted spoon. Cook pasta in same water until al dente, about 8 minutes.

- Drain pasta, reserving 1/2 cup cooking water. Add pasta to sauce; toss over medium heat, adding enough reserved pasta cooking water to coat the pasta with sauce.

Candied Apricots and Sweet Cheese Bites

Most supermarket delis carry a range of cheese that is nice for this; have them slice the cheese for you.

8 fat Australian candied apricots
2 (1/4- to 1/3-inch-thick) slices cream havarti or other sweet cheese such as domestic muenster or fresh goat cheese or ricotta

- Cut apricots in half horizontally. Cut out 4 rounds the size of apricots from each cheese slice using a cookie cutter. Sandwich cheese between apricot halves. Serve as is or cut into quarters and skewer with decorative picks.

Makes 4 to 6 servings.

Virtual-Island-Vacation Supper

• Quesadilla Grande • Poached Salmon Medallions with Guacamole • *Marinated Three-Bean Salad* • Passionate Pineapple Parfaits

MAKES 4 SERVINGS

Here's a quick and delicious psychological boost when you can't get away or just want to kindle memories of a good time in the sun.

GAME PLAN

1. Preheat oven. Assemble parfaits except for topping; freeze.
2. Assemble quesadilla. Heat poaching liquid.
3. Poach fish. Bake quesadilla.

Quesadilla Grande

2 (14-inch) tomato-basil sandwich wraps
2 cups shredded sharp cheddar cheese
1 bunch thin green onions, trimmed, finely chopped

• Preheat oven to 425°. Place one wrap on foil-lined baking sheet; sprinkle with cheese and onions. Top with remaining wrap; place in middle of oven even if oven is not up to temperature. Bake until cheese starts to melt, 3 minutes.

• Turn over quesadilla using your fingers (it's not too hot.) Bake until cheese melts, about 3 minutes. Slide quesadilla onto cutting board; using pizza cutter, cut into irregular 2-inch pieces. (For 16 nice-sized pieces, cut 4 even rows in each direction.)

Poached Salmon Medallions with Guacamole

3/4 cup dry white wine

3/4 cup water

1/2 cup coarsely chopped celery leaves

1 teaspoon low-sodium soy sauce or 1/2 teaspoon salt

2 (12-ounce) salmon steaks, 1-inch-thick, skinned, filleted, and shaped into medallions (see note below)

1 cup guacamole (store-bought or homemade)

4 lemon twists

• Combine wine, water, celery, and soy sauce in deep medium skillet; add medallions. Heat to simmering over medium heat; cover and cook 3 minutes. Remove pan from heat; turn medallions; let medallions stand, covered, until almost cooked through, about 5 minutes.

• To serve: Remove medallions to paper towels and blot dry. Place on platter; top each with a mound of guacamole and then a lemon twist.

Note: To make medallions, use a sharp paring knife to remove skin and bones from fish, trying not to tear the flesh (this is easy if your knife is sharp). Divide each steak into 2 pieces at natural division in thickest part. Wrap thin end around thicker part of each to make a solid round; secure with wooden picks.

Passionate Pineapple Parfaits

You can use any type of granola mix—or cookie or cake crumbs instead of granola—any type of fruits, and any flavor sorbet, gelato, or ice cream.

1 cup tropical-mix granola

1/2 pint passion-fruit sorbet

1 (81/4-ounce) can crushed pineapple or 1/2 cup chopped fresh pineapple

1 large kiwifruit, peeled, cut crosswise into 8 slices

aerosol whipped-cream topping or sweetened whipped cream

• Layer in each of 4 wine glasses: 2 tablespoons granola, 2 tablespoons sorbet, 2 tablespoons pineapple and juice, 1 kiwi slice, 2 tablespoons sorbet, and 2 tablespoons granola. Pipe a nice rosette of topping to fill each glass and garnish with remaining kiwi.

Southern Sunday Dinner

• Tupelo Honey-Roasted Pork Tenderloin • Sweet Potatoes in Star Anise Broth • Quick Coconut Cake

MAKES 4 SERVINGS

The midday meal in the American South was traditionally called dinner (with supper to follow). Nowadays "lunch" has entered the vernacular, but it's still called dinner when you have it on Sunday.

GAME PLAN

1. Preheat broiler. Coat pork; broil.
2. Turn pork. Make anise broth. Lower oven rack.
3. Make cake; refrigerate. Heat potatoes.

Tupelo Honey-Roasted Pork Tenderloin

nonstick cooking spray

1 (1 1/4-pound) pork tenderloin, at room temperature, trimmed of silverskin and excess fat

1/4 cup tupelo or other strong-flavored honey

1/4 cup soy sauce

1 tablespoon Dijon mustard

1/4 teaspoon garlic powder

• Preheat broiler. Line a roasting pan with foil; grease with cooking spray. Place tenderloin in pan.

• Mix remaining ingredients in cup; brush over tenderloin. Broil 4 inches from heat source, turning tenderloin every 2 minutes, until browned on all sides, 6 minutes in all.

• Lower oven rack one notch so pork is 6 inches from heat. Broil tenderloin until internal temperature reaches 145°, 6 to 8 minutes. Cover with foil and let stand 5 minutes.

Sweet Potatoes in Star Anise Broth

1 tablespoon all-purpose flour

2 (16-ounce) cans sweet potatoes

2 star anise

1 cup orange juice

2 tablespoons honey

2 tablespoons rice wine

salt to taste

● Place flour in 2-quart saucepan; gradually drain potato liquid into flour, whisking until blended. Add star anise, orange juice, honey, and rice wine; heat to boiling over medium heat, whisking constantly. Boil 1 minute. Reduce heat and simmer 5 minutes.

● Discard star anise; add sweet potatoes and heat through. Season with salt.

Makes 4 to 6 servings.

Quick Coconut Cake

1 store-bought sponge cake layer or 4 store-bought sponge short cakes (near the berries in the produce department)

1 cup sweetened flaked coconut

1 (8-ounce) container sour cream

1/2 cup sugar

1/2 teaspoon vanilla extract

● Cut cake in half to make 2 layers. Combine coconut, sour cream, sugar, and vanilla in a medium bowl. Whisk until blended. Spread half the mixture over one half of the wide cake or over the cut side of the thick cake. Cover with remaining cake; spread coconut mixture on top. Cover and refrigerate until serving. (Coconut mixture will thicken as it stands and also soak into the cake.) Cut into wedges to serve.

Makes 4 to 6 servings.

"Who Really Needs a Villa?" Feast

• Tuscan Squab • Penne with Pesto, Porcini, and Peas
• Cauliflower with Anchovy-Caper Sauce • *Favorite Gelato*

MAKES 4 SERVINGS

The delicious flavors of Tuscany can be conjured up in a flash when you have the right creative mindset and a quick cook's strategy.

GAME PLAN

1. Heat water for pasta and cauliflower. Soak porcini. Cook squab. Make cauliflower sauce.
2. Cook pasta and cauliflower. Strain and slice porcini. Turn squab.
3. Mix cauliflower with sauce. Toss pasta and peas with pesto and cheeses.

Tuscan Squab

4 semiboneless (backbones and 2 outer wing joints removed) squab (young pigeons) or small cornish hens

3 tablespoons olive oil or vegetable oil

1 teaspoon kosher salt

1 teaspoon lemon-pepper seasoning

• Flatten each squab with your hand to crack breast keel bone. Rinse and pat dry. Make small slits in skin on both sides of tails; tuck legs into slits.

• Heat stovetop griddle (large enough to cover two burners) or two heavy skillets over medium-high heat. Brush breast sides of squab with oil and sprinkle with salt and pepper. When pan is hot, reduce heat to medium; place squab, breast sides down, in pan(s) above each burner. Place foil-covered flat bricks or roasting pans weighted with cans on top of squab.

• Cook squab until they start to brown, 8 minutes. Remove weights. Brush back sides with oil and sprinkle with salt and pepper. Turn squab over with tongs. Replace weights and cook squab until done, 6 minutes more.

169

Penne with Pesto, Porcini, and Peas

Double the recipe for a vegetarian main course.

salt
1 ounce dried porcini mushrooms
1 cup very hot water
8 ounces penne
1 (10-ounce) package frozen peas
4 tablespoons pesto (store-bought or see
  recipe page 213)
1 cup grated Parmigiano-Reggiano cheese
4 ounces ricotta salata or blue cheese
freshly ground pepper to taste

• Heat 2 quarts salted water to boiling in large deep skillet. Meanwhile, soak mushrooms in very hot water in a bowl until soft, about 10 minutes.

• Cook pasta in boiling water until al dente, 8 minutes, adding peas during the last 5 minutes of cooking.

• Drain mushrooms through cheesecloth-lined sieve (to remove sand) placed over a bowl. Rinse mushrooms, slice, and add to strained liquid; add pesto.

• Drain pasta and peas, reserving 1/2 cup cooking liquid. Return pasta and peas to pan, add pesto mixture and toss over medium heat. Add Parmigiano-Reggiano and toss. Crumble ricotta salata on top and season with pepper. Toss again with enough reserved pasta cooking water to coat the pasta evenly.

Cauliflower with Anchovy-Caper Sauce

If you're not an anchovy fan, substitute the juice of a lemon, preferably a Meyer lemon.

salt
1 pound cauliflower florets (from 1 small head)
10 oil-packed anchovies, mashed with 2 tablespoons
  packing oil
1/4 cup drained brined capers
1/2 teaspoon crushed red-pepper flakes
2 tablespoons torn fresh parsley leaves

• Heat 2 quarts salted water to boiling in large deep skillet. Add florets; cook until tender, 2 to 3 minutes.

• Place remaining ingredients in serving bowl; add 1/3 cup cauliflower cooking water and mix. Drain florets; add to sauce and toss.

Steak Lover's Delight

• Beef with Peppercorn Sauce • Kasha with Bow-Tie Pasta • Mizuna with Roasted Onions

MAKES 4 SERVINGS

This hearty dinner comes alive with the flavors of spicy peppercorns and the richness of the side dishes.

GAME PLAN

1. Heat water for pasta. Sauté vegetables for kasha; cook kasha.
2. Cook pasta. Prepare mizuna; keep warm.
3. Prepare and pan-fry steaks; make sauce.

Beef with Peppercorn Sauce

2 tablespoons all-purpose flour

1 tablespoon coarsely ground black pepper

1 tablespoon crushed dried green peppercorns

1 teaspoon kosher salt or more to taste

4 (8-ounce) strip steaks, at room temperature

1 tablespoon unsalted butter

1 tablespoon olive oil

2 shallots, minced

1 cup low-sodium beef, chicken, or vegetable broth

1 tablespoon drained green peppercorns in brine or crushed dried green peppercorns

• Mix flour, black pepper, dried peppercorns, and 1 teaspoon salt on a plate. Dredge steaks in mixture, shake off excess.

• Melt butter in oil in a large heavy skillet over high heat. Add steaks and sear on both sides. Lower heat and cook to desired doneness, about 4 minutes total for medium-rare.

• Remove steaks to a heated platter and cover loosely with foil to keep warm. Add shallots to pan; sauté 1 minute. Add broth and boil over high heat, scraping up browned bits, until reduced by two thirds. Stir in brined peppercorns. Taste and adjust seasoning if needed. Pour sauce over steaks and serve at once.

Kasha with Bow-Tie Pasta

The nutty taste of the crushed buckwheat grains (kasha) is partnered with pasta for a subtle contrast of flavors and textures.

salt
3 tablespoons unsalted butter
1 cup chopped red onion
1 small red bell pepper, seeded, finely chopped
1 cup whole kasha
2 cups vegetable broth, chicken broth, or water
2 cups bow-tie pasta

- Heat 2 quarts salted water to boiling in a large deep skillet. Melt butter in a large skillet over medium-high heat. Add onion, bell pepper, and kasha; sauté until onion starts to soften, about 3 minutes. Add broth; heat to boiling. Reduce heat and simmer, mostly covered, until kasha is softened, about 10 minutes.

- Meanwhile, cook pasta in the boiling water until al dente, about 10 minutes. Drain pasta; stir into kasha mixture.

Makes 4 to 6 servings.

Mizuna with Roasted Onions

8 marinated roasted cipollini (flat Italian onions)
or other marinated (not pickled) onions
plus 1/4 cup marinade from onions
8 cups rinsed, dried mizuna or arugula
freshly ground pepper to taste
wedge of Parmigiano-Reggiano cheese

- Halve onions lengthwise. Heat marinade in medium skillet over medium-high heat. Add onions, partially cover and heat through, about 2 minutes. Add mizuna and season with pepper. Stir to coat leaves with marinade. Heat through, about 2 minutes. Spoon onto plates; shave curls of cheese on top using a vegetable peeler.

Family-Style Flavors

• Skillet-Barbecued Chicken with Peppers • *Pork and Beans* • Mom's Grilled Peaches • Cookie and Ice Cream Sandwiches

MAKES 4 SERVINGS

Here's a meal for nights when everyone is on the go—but something home-cooked is still important.

GAME PLAN

1. Preheat broiler. Sauté peppers and add chicken and sauce.
2. Assemble ice-cream sandwiches; freeze.
3. Heat pork and beans. Grill peaches.

Skillet-Barbecued Chicken with Peppers

1 tablespoon vegetable oil

1 red bell pepper, seeded, slivered

1 yellow bell pepper, seeded, slivered

1 orange bell pepper, seeded, slivered

slivered meat from 1 (2 1/2-pound) roasted chicken
   (about 2 1/2 cups)

1 cup prepared barbecue sauce

1/2 cup beer

rolls for serving (optional)

• Heat oil in large nonstick skillet over high heat. Add peppers; sauté until softened, 2 minutes. Stir in chicken, barbecue sauce, and beer. Cover; simmer over medium heat 10 minutes. If desired, serve on rolls.

Mom's Grilled Peaches

4 canned or fresh white or yellow peach halves

*4 teaspoons grape jelly or fancy red or purple
    preserves*

● Preheat broiler. Line broiler pan with foil. Place peaches cut side up in pan and spoon jelly into center. Broil 6 inches from heat source until tops are browned and peaches are heated through, about 6 minutes.

Cookie and Ice-Cream Sandwiches

1 pint vanilla or your favorite flavor ice cream

8 (3-inch) flat cookies such as chocolate wafers

● Soften ice cream until scoopable but not melting. Using a spatula, place 1/3 cup ice cream on the flat sides of 4 cookies and spread just to the edges. Cover each with a remaining cookie, flat side down. Press each sandwich together just enough so that cookies do not break. Serve immediately or freeze until serving.

Fusion Italian Dinner

• Steamed Chicken Rolls • Pappardelle alla Vodka • Broccoli with Lemon-Garlic Crumbs

MAKES 4 SERVINGS

The wok comes in so handy for many cooking methods and all cuisines. If you have a set of stacked steamer baskets, cook the chicken rolls and the broccoli at the same time.

GAME PLAN

1. Heat water for pasta. Make vodka sauce; keep warm.
2. Assemble chicken rolls; steam. Cook pasta.
3. Cook broccoli and crumbs. Toss pasta with sauce.

Steamed Chicken Rolls

4 thin (but not paper-thin) slices prosciutto di Parma
lemon-herb or lemon-pepper seasoning to taste
8 leaves fresh basil, stacked, slivered
4 (6-ounce) thin chicken cutlets
kosher salt to taste
2 cups cleaned baby spinach
4 ounces smoked mozzarella, thinly sliced
16 chives (optional)
1/4 cup chicken broth or water

• Prepare wok or wide steamer with boiling water. Place prosciutto on work surface; sprinkle with seasoning and basil. Top each with a cutlet, a light dusting of salt and seasoning, a layer of spinach and then the mozzarella. Roll up, jelly-roll fashion. Tie each roll with 4 chives spaced at even intervals or secure with wooden toothpicks. Trim off excess chive.

• Place rolls in shallow bowl and sprinkle with broth. Place bowl in wok or steamer rack over boiling water. Cover and steam until cheese starts to ooze out, 6 to 8 minutes. (Carefully remove lid to check the progress after 6 minutes.)

• Cool chicken 5 minutes. Cut each roll crosswise at an angle in between chives to make 4 pieces or remove toothpicks and slice. Drizzle with steaming juices.

Pappardelle alla Vodka

salt
1 (15-ounce) can tomato sauce
1 cup heavy cream
2 tablespoons vodka or more to taste
1 tablespoon chopped chipotles in adobo sauce
   or more to taste
8 ounces pappardelle pasta, broken into
   2-inch pieces
freshly ground pepper to taste
torn fresh mint, basil, or parsley, or a mix for serving

• Heat 2 quarts salted water in deep large skillet to boiling. Meanwhile, whisk tomato sauce, cream, vodka, and chipotles in large nonstick skillet over medium-high heat until boiling.

• Cook pasta in boiling water until al dente, about 6 minutes. Drain, reserving 1/2 cup pasta cooking water. Add pasta to sauce; stir and add enough pasta water to coat pasta evenly. Taste sauce and season with salt and pepper. Sprinkle with mint.

Broccoli with Lemon-Garlic Crumbs

1 cup herb stuffing mix
2 tablespoons unsalted butter
1 teaspoon lemon-pepper seasoning
1/2 teaspoon garlic salt
2 cups broccoli florets

• Crush stuffing mix in plastic food storage bag with your hand to make coarse crumbs. Melt butter in medium skillet over medium-high heat. Add crumbs and seasonings and sauté until hot and coated. Remove to dish; cover.

• Pour 1/2 inch water into same pan; heat to boiling over medium-high heat. Add broccoli and cover. Steam until tender-crisp or desired doneness, 5 to 8 minutes. Remove to serving dish; top with crumbs.

Elegant Woodsy Flavors

- **Pheasant Breasts with Calvados Cream Sauce**
- **Sautéed Mushrooms • Crème de Menthe Parfaits**

MAKES 4 SERVINGS

This actually is a French-inspired menu, and that may or may not add cachet—as if the pheasant isn't enough. Feel free to add your favorite hooch if you don't have Calvados, the distinctive, dry apple brandy of Normandy.

GAME PLAN

1. Cook pheasant breasts. Assemble parfaits without topping and freeze.
2. Sauté mushrooms and keep warm.
3. Make sauce for pheasant. Garnish parfaits before serving.

Pheasant Breasts with Calvados Cream Sauce

4 pheasant breast halves from 2 (2 1/2- to 3-pound)
  pheasants (see Note)
fine sea salt and freshly ground pepper to taste
2 tablespoons unsalted butter
2 tablespoons vegetable oil
12 sprigs fresh thyme
2 shallots, finely chopped
1/2 cup heavy cream
1/4 cup Calvados
1/4 cup dried apples, chopped

• Season breast halves with salt and pepper. Melt butter in oil in a large skillet over medium-high heat; fry thyme sprigs 1 minute. Place breasts skin side down over thyme; cook until well browned, about 4 minutes. Turn and cook through, about 4 minutes more. Remove to warm platter; cover with foil.

• Add shallots to pan and sauté 3 minutes. Increase heat to high and add cream, Calvados, and apples, scraping up browned bits. Boil until reduced to 1/3 cup; serve with pheasant breasts.

Note: Remove breasts with bones attached from pheasants and split each in half. Remove pinions and second wing joints. Use remaining carcasses for stock.

Sautéed Mushrooms

2 tablespoons unsalted butter
12 ounces sliced mushrooms (any kind or a mix)
1/4 teaspoon garlic salt or powder or 1 clove garlic,
*   crushed through a press*
salt and freshly ground pepper to taste
juice of 1 lemon or 1/4 cup Madeira, vermouth, or
*   table wine*

● Melt butter in large nonstick skillet over medium-high heat. Add mushrooms and garlic salt and sauté until tender, 2 minutes. Remove to a bowl; season well with salt and pepper. Add lemon juice to hot pan; stir, scraping up browned bits. Add sauce to mushrooms and serve at room temperature, or add mushrooms to sauce, reheat and serve hot.

Crème de Menthe Parfaits

Once you start making parfaits, you may never bake again! Long-handled ice-tea spoons and an inexpensive set of parfait glasses will add to the festive presentation and make the eating, even when spiked with a jewel-colored cordial, a kid-like joy. You can always use the crimson, black currant-flavored crème de cassis instead of the mint liqueur.

3/4 cup green crème de menthe
1 pint best-quality vanilla ice cream, softened
aerosol whipped-cream topping or sweetened
*   whipped cream*
maraschino cherries with a stem

● Spoon 1 1/2 tablespoons crème de menthe into the bottom of each of 4 parfait glasses or sturdy pilsner glasses. Add a scoop of ice cream to each and press down on the ice cream with the back of a spoon just hard enough to make the crème de menthe swirl up the glass. Repeat with remaining crème de menthe and ice cream.

● Pipe nice rosettes of topping to fill the glasses or rise above the glass and garnish with cherries. Serve immediately.

Note: To make ahead, assemble the parfaits without the topping up to 3 hours before serving and freeze. To serve, let stand at room temperature just long enough to soften the ice cream and garnish with the topping and cherry.

Dinner with a Fiery Finish

• Broiled Garlic-Mustard Lamb Chops • Curried Cauliflower Purée • *House Salad with Favorite Dressing* • Cherries Jubilee

MAKES 4 SERVINGS

Here's that impress the boss, the in-laws, or your date menu everyone needs to master. The main course is elegant and the dessert will long be remembered.

GAME PLAN

1. Preheat broiler. Cook florets. Rub chops with garlic mixture.
2. Purée florets and keep warm. Assemble cherries jubilee. Make salad.
3. Broil chops. Heat cherries at dessert time.

Broiled Garlic-Mustard Lamb Chops

1 large garlic clove, crushed through a press

1 tablespoon olive oil

1 tablespoon grainy prepared mustard

1/2 teaspoon freshly ground pepper

8 (6-ounce) rib lamb chops (1- to 1 1/4-inch-thick)

• Preheat broiler. Mix garlic, oil, mustard, and pepper; rub over chops. Place chops on rack in broiler pan. Broil 3 inches from heat source, 3 to 4 minutes each side for medium-rare. Serve on warm plates.

Curried Cauliflower Purée

1 pound cauliflower florets

1/2 cup water

1 tablespoon unsalted butter, softened, plus extra
   for serving, if desired

1 teaspoon hot curry powder (such as Madras)

1/4 teaspoon salt

pinch of ground white pepper

• Halve the florets lengthwise. Bring the water to a boil in a 1-quart saucepan over medium-high heat. Add florets, cover, and cook until tender, about 5 minutes.

• Drain the florets, reserving cooking water, and place in food processor. Add 1/4 cup cooking water, the butter, curry powder, salt, and pepper. Purée until desired consistency, adding more cooking liquid or more butter, in pieces, to reach desired consistency.

Cherries Jubilee

2 cups drained jarred cherries, canned pitted
   cherries, or thawed, frozen cherries

1/4 cup kirschwasser (cherry brandy)

2 tablespoons fresh lemon juice

1/4 to 1/2 cup sugar

vanilla ice cream

2 tablespoons unsalted butter, in small bits

1/2 cup brandy

• Mix cherries, kirschwasser, lemon juice, and sugar to taste (how much sugar will depend on the kind of cherries) in a large, heavy skillet. Let stand at least 10 minutes or until ready to serve.

• To serve: Have the ice cream sitting in heat-safe dishes on the table. Heat cherry mixture to boiling over medium-high heat. Stir in butter and heat until melted. Add brandy and heat to almost boiling. Quickly take skillet to the table. Using a long match, ignite the brandy at the near edge of the skillet. Spoon sauce and cherries, flaming, over the ice cream.

Dinner for Restless Palates

• Sweet-and-Sour Lychee Pork Kebabs • Quinoa Surprise • Cucumber and Mint Raita

MAKES 4 SERVINGS

No same old, same old here! The bright, juicy, crunchy, tangy, fragrant components will have your guests racing through a thesaurus to compliment the cook.

GAME PLAN
1. Preheat broiler. Start cooking quinoa. Marinate pork.
2. Make dipping sauce and raita.
3. Broil kebabs. Finish quinoa.

Sweet-and-Sour Lychee Pork Kebabs

1 pound lean pork, cut into 3/4-inch cubes

2 tablespoons sesame oil

2 tablespoon fresh lemon or lime juice

2 tablespoons soy sauce

2 tablespoons cornstarch

1 (11-ounce) can lychees, drained, juice reserved

1 (14-ounce) can pineapple chunks, drained, juice reserved

1 tablespoon wine vinegar

2 tablespoons rice flour

1 red bell pepper, seeded, cut into 1/2-inch squares

4 green onions, trimmed, cut into 1-inch pieces

• Preheat broiler. Line broiler pan with foil. Combine pork, oil, juice, and 1 tablespoon soy sauce in bowl and toss well. Let marinate 5 minutes. Meanwhile, make dipping sauce: Blend remaining soy sauce and cornstarch in saucepan; whisk in lychee and pineapple juices and vinegar. Set aside.

• Sprinkle pork with rice flour; toss. Thread pork, lychees, pineapple, pepper, and onions onto 4 (8-inch) metal skewers in alternating order. Broil 4 inches from heat source, turning after 4 minutes, until pork is browned and sizzling, 8 minutes.

• While kebabs cook, heat dipping sauce to boiling, stirring. Simmer 1 minute, until thickened. Serve with kebabs.

Quinoa Surprise

1 cup quinoa

2 cups hot vegetable or chicken broth (from bouillon
cubes is fine)

3 tablespoons unsalted butter

1/4 cup chopped cashews

1/4 cup golden mustard seeds

1/2 teaspoon crushed red-pepper flakes

salt to taste

• Place quinoa in fine sieve; rinse well. Place in 2-quart saucepan. Add broth; heat to boiling over medium-high heat. Reduce heat to medium-low and simmer until quinoa is tender, about 15 minutes.

• While quinoa cooks, melt butter in small skillet over medium heat. Add cashews, mustard seeds, and pepper flakes; immediately cover pan. Cook until mustard seeds pop actively against the lid. (Do not get curious and lift the lid or you will have a real mess.) Remove pan from heat and set aside until popping stops, about 5 minutes.

• Stir mustard seed mixture into quinoa. Season with salt if needed.

Makes 4 to 6 servings.

Cucumber and Mint Raita

1 cup plain yogurt

1 Kirby cucumber, finely diced

2 tablespoon finely chopped or torn fresh mint leaves

1/2 teaspoon salt

1/4 teaspoon freshly ground pepper

• Combine ingredients in bowl and mix well.

Under the Spanish Sun

• Skillet-Braised Fish Steaks
• Patatas Pobres (Poor Man's Potatoes) • Sangría

MAKES 4 SERVINGS

Spanish cuisine has always distinguished itself, but now it's in the spotlight on the international culinary stage like never before. Here are some classic basics for a weekend meal.

GAME PLAN
1. Start potatoes. Coat fish.
2. Turn potatoes. Cook fish.
3. Make sangría.

Skillet-Braised Fish Steaks

4 (6- to 8-ounce) fish steaks, about 1 inch thick
   (cod, scrod, or tuna are nice)
salt and freshly ground pepper to taste
1/4 cup all-purpose flour
1/2 teaspoon smoked Spanish paprika or hot
   Hungarian paprika
2 tablespoons unsalted butter
1 tablespoon olive oil
1 (14 1/2-ounce) can stewed or chopped tomatoes
   (roasted garlic or other flavors are fine)
1/2 cup dry white wine
1 tablespoon red-wine vinegar

• Sprinkle fish steaks on both sides with salt and pepper. Place flour on waxed paper; mix in paprika. Dredge steaks in flour mixture; shake off excess.

• Melt butter in oil in large heavy nonstick skillet over medium-high heat. When foam subsides, add steaks and cook until browned on both sides, about 5 minutes in all. Remove to a plate.

• Add tomatoes, wine, and vinegar to skillet; stir, scraping up browned bits. Heat to boiling. Taste sauce and adjust seasoning if needed. Return steaks to pan and cover. Reduce heat to medium and simmer until steaks are cooked through, about 5 minutes longer.

Patatas Pobres (Poor Man's Potatoes)

3 tablespoons olive oil

1 (1 1/4-pound) pouch refrigerated sliced
  potatoes or 4 medium all-purpose potatoes, cut
  into 1/8-inch-thick rounds

kosher salt to taste

2 tablespoons water

1 large garlic clove, minced

2 tablespoons torn or chopped fresh parsley leaves

● Heat oil in large heavy nonstick skillet over medium-high heat until hot. Spread out potatoes in pan and turn to coat with oil. Sprinkle with salt. Cover; cook over medium heat, lifting and turning potatoes occasionally and adjusting heat to brown potatoes evenly and quickly, 10 minutes.

● Sprinkle water around edge of pan. Cover and steam potatoes until tender and water has evaporated, about 5 minutes. Sprinkle with garlic and parsley.

Sangría

1 (25-ounce) bottle dry red wine, chilled

1/2 cup frozen peach slices

1/2 cup frozen strawberries

1/2 cup frozen blueberries

1 (6-ounce) can frozen lemonade

● Mix ingredients in a large pitcher.

Dinner with Sand Between Your Toes

• Grilled Soft-Shell Crabs Margarita • Grilled Bluefish Fillets with Citrus Squeeze • Southern-Fried Okra • *Ice-Cold Watermelon Chunks*

MAKES 4 SERVINGS

When the days are long and weekends extra fun, get the grill going with a barbecue on the beach.

GAME PLAN
1. Prepare grill or preheat broiler.
2. Coat okra. Prepare crabs and fish.
3. Grill or broil crabs and fish; fry okra.

Grilled Soft-Shell Crabs Margarita

8 soft-shell crabs
1/2 cup bottled margarita mix
1/3 cup olive oil
1/4 cup green salsa fresca or bottled salsa
2 tablespoons tequila

• Prepare charcoal or gas grill or preheat broiler. Place crabs in baking dish. Mix margarita mix, oil, salsa, and tequila in a bowl; pour half the mixture over the crabs. Turn to coat. Refrigerate until grilling.

• Grill or broil crabs 3 to 4 inches from heat source just until cooked through, 2 to 3 minutes each side. Heat remaining margarita sauce in bowl in microwave or in a small skillet until hot.

• Remove crabs to serving platter; drizzle with remaining margarita sauce.

Grilled Bluefish Fillets with Citrus Squeeze

2 pounds bluefish fillets (2 large or 4 small), skinned
2 blood oranges, one halved, one quartered
2 Meyer lemons, one halved, one quartered
2 limes, one halved, one quartered
1/4 cup mayonnaise
salt to taste
crushed dried green peppercorns to taste
1/4 cup fresh cilantro leaves

● Prepare charcoal or gas grill or preheat broiler. Place fillets skinned side down in oiled fish grill or in foil-lined roasting pan. (Place fish grill on baking sheet.)

● Squeeze the juice from the citrus halves over the fish. Slather the fish with mayonnaise and sprinkle with salt and peppercorns. Close grill and clamp handle if using fish grill. Grill or broil fish 4 inches from heat source until cooked through, 6 to 9 minutes, according to thickness of fish. (If fish starts to brown too much before it is cooked through, move fish farther from heat source.)

● Sprinkle fish with cilantro. Serve with citrus quarters for squeezing.

Southern-Fried Okra

1 pound okra, thick stem ends trimmed, pods cut
  into 1/2-inch rounds
salt
1 1/2 cups fine yellow or white cornmeal
1/4 teaspoon black pepper
vegetable oil for frying

● Preheat oven to 300°. Place okra in bowl of salted ice water. Soak 5 minutes. Line baking sheet with paper towels. Mix cornmeal with 1/2 teaspoon salt and the pepper in a plastic food storage bag.

● Heat 1/2 inch oil in large skillet over medium-high heat to shimmering. Drain okra. In batches, shake okra in cornmeal mixture to coat; shake off excess. Fry okra in oil until golden brown, about 2 minutes per batch. Place fried okra on prepared baking sheet and keep warm in oven while coating and frying remaining okra.

A Showcase of Simple Flavors

• Carrot-Tomato Soup • Pan-Grilled Veal Chops with Taleggio and Frizzled Sage • Fettuccine with Mixed Summer Squashes

MAKES 4 SERVINGS

The chop's the thing that makes this a meal for a special occasion, such as a welcome home for family or a bon voyage to friends.

GAME PLAN

1. Heat water for pasta. Start soup in microwave. Stuff and brown chops.
2. Purée soup. Cook squash and pasta.
3. Deglaze pan from chops; frizzle sage. Make squash sauce; toss with pasta.

Carrot-Tomato Soup

4 to 5 cups chicken broth (homemade or made from 2 small chicken bouillon cubes)

3 tablespoons sun-dried tomato paste or regular tomato paste

1 (10-ounce) package shredded carrots or 2 cups peeled baby carrots, finely chopped in a food processor

1/2 teaspoon dried thyme or dill weed plus extra for serving

salt and freshly ground pepper to taste

2 tablespoons unsalted butter, in 4 pats

• Mix 1/2 cup broth and tomato paste in large microwave-safe bowl until blended. Cover with microwave-safe plastic wrap; cook on high power until boiling, about 1 minute. Add carrots, 1 cup broth, thyme, and salt; cover, vent, and cook on high until carrots are tender, about 5 minutes. Carefully purée in blender; pour into 2-quart saucepan.

• Rinse out blender with 1 cup broth; add to saucepan. Add enough broth to make soup of desired consistency. Heat to boiling; season with salt and pepper. Ladle into bowls; add a pat of butter to each and stir to make a melted-butter swirl. Sprinkle each serving with a pinch of thyme.

Pan-Grilled Veal Chops with Taleggio and Frizzled Sage

4 (3/4-inch-thick) bone-in rib veal chops, at room
    temperature
2 thin (but but not paper-thin) slices prosciutto
    di Parma
4 ounces young (semisoft) Taleggio cheese, cut into
    4 slices
12 fresh sage leaves, shredded
kosher salt and freshly ground black pepper to taste
4 tablespoons unsalted butter
3 tablespoon olive oil
1/3 cup dry white vermouth or wine

• Cut a deep horizontal pocket in the side of each chop. Cut prosciutto slices crosswise in half; top with slices of cheese and pinches of sage. Roll up and insert into pockets. Sprinkle chops on both sides with salt and pepper.

• Melt 2 tablespoons butter in the oil in a large heavy skillet over medium-high heat; add the chops (they should not be crowded; use 2 pans if necessary). Cook until browned, 1 to 2 minutes. Turn and cook until cheese starts to melt, 2 to 3 minutes. Remove to a platter; cover with foil and keep warm.

• Add wine to skillet; stir, scraping up browned bits. Boil to reduce to 2 tablespoons, about 2 minutes. Pour over chops; cover again. Melt remaining butter in pan; add remaining sage and fry until sage is crisp and butter is browned, 2 minutes. Pour over chops.

Fettuccine with Mixed Summer Squashes

salt
1 medium zucchini, sliced into thin rounds
1 medium yellow summer squash, sliced into
    thin rounds
8 ounces fresh fettuccine
1/4 cup extra-virgin olive oil
1/2 teaspoon crushed red-pepper flakes
1/2 teaspoon garlic-pepper or lemon-pepper seasoning
1/2 cup shredded Asiago or Pecorino Romano cheese
1/4 cup mixed imported olives in herbs, pitted if you
    have time (optional)
1/4 cup torn fresh parsley leaves

• Heat 3 quarts salted water to boiling in a large deep skillet. Add zucchini and squash and cook until tender, about 3 minutes. Remove with slotted spoon to strainer placed over a bowl. Add pasta to squash cooking water; cook until al dente, 4 to 6 minutes.

• Meanwhile, heat oil in another deep skillet over medium-high heat. Add pepper flakes; sauté until sizzling, 1 minute. Add zucchini, squash (reserve draining liquid), and seasoning. Stir and keep warm over medium heat.

• Drain pasta; add to squash mixture and toss to mix over medium heat. Add cheese, olives, and parsley and toss with enough squash liquid to make a creamy sauce as the cheese melts. Taste and add more salt if needed.

Midsummer Twilight Supper

• Pecan-Crusted Chicken Cutlets • Curried Apricot Sauce • Warm Rice Salad

MAKES 4 SERVINGS

Deconstruct a chicken curry dinner and you have this homey spread to enjoy under emerging stars.

GAME PLAN

1. Start rice. Preheat oven.
2. Make sauce.
3. Coat and fry cutlets.

Pecan-Crusted Chicken Cutlets

1/4 cup all-purpose flour

1/2 teaspoon salt

1/4 teaspoon freshly ground pepper

1 egg beaten with 2 tablespoons water

1 1/2 cups ground pecans

4 (6-ounce) thin chicken cutlets

2 tablespoons unsalted butter

2 tablespoons safflower or other vegetable oil

Curried Apricot Sauce (recipe follows)

• Preheat oven to 300°. Mix flour, salt, and pepper on plate. Place egg mixture in shallow bowl. Place pecans on plate. Dredge cutlets in flour mixture, shake off excess. Coat with egg mixture; drain off excess; dip into pecans, patting to help them to stick.

• Melt 1 tablespoon butter in 1 tablespoon oil in large nonstick skillet over medium heat. Add 2 cutlets; cover and cook until browned, for 3 minutes. Turn cutlets and cook, covered, until browned. Remove to shallow baking dish. Keep cutlets warm in oven while cooking remaining cutlets with remaining butter and oil. Serve with apricot sauce.

Curried Apricot Sauce

1 tablespoon vegetable oil
1 shallot, finely chopped
1 teaspoon curry powder
1/4 cup red wine
2 tablespoons apricot preserves
1 cup mayonnaise
fresh lemon juice to taste

• Heat oil in small skillet over medium-high heat. Add shallot and sauté until tender, about 3 minutes. Stir in curry powder and cook 1 minute. Add wine and preserves and stir until blended. Cook 1 minute. Remove pan from heat and stir in mayonnaise. Season with lemon juice.

Warm Rice Salad

1 cup rice
2 cups water
1/2 cup fresh peas
1/4 cup herb vinaigrette (store-bought or see recipe page 216) or more to taste
1/2 cup diced cucumber

• Rinse rice and place in small saucepan. Add water and heat to boiling. Reduce heat and simmer 15 minutes; add peas and toss. Cover; let stand 3 minutes.

• Spoon rice into serving bowl. Sprinkle with vinaigrette and cucumber; toss with wooden salad forks.

Lip-Smacking Shrimpfest

• Stir-Fried Harissa Shrimp in Shells • Chinese Noodle Pancake • Crunchy Fruit Bouchées

MAKES 4 SERVINGS

The hot chili sauce called *harissa* is available from Middle Eastern grocery stores. It's one of those ingredients that, like sambal oelek, you'll be glad you discovered and use in soups, stews, couscous, dips, etc.

GAME PLAN
1. Preheat oven. Heat water for noodles. Freeze fruit.
2. Cook noodles; drain and season. Fry pancake; keep warm.
3. Coat fruit. Stir-fry shrimp.

Stir-Fried Harissa Shrimp in Shells

2 tablespoons vegetable oil

1 1/2 pounds raw unpeeled jumbo shrimp
   (tails intact)

1 bunch thin green onions, trimmed, cut into
   1-inch pieces

1 medium yellow bell pepper, seeded, thinly sliced

1 cup shredded carrots

2 tablespoons harissa (Tunisian pepper paste; store-
   bought or see recipe page 214), or more to taste

2 tablespoons low-sodium soy sauce

2 tablespoons water

• Heat wok or large heavy skillet over medium-high heat. Add oil and when almost smoking, add shrimp, onions, pepper, and carrots. Stir-fry 2 minutes using long chopsticks or Chinese stir-fry shovel.

• Add harissa, soy sauce, and water. Stir-fry until shrimp are pink and curled, 1 to 2 minutes.

Chinese Noodle Pancake

12 ounces fresh Hong Kong–style egg noodles
  (available in Asian markets)
1 tablespoon low-sodium soy sauce or more to taste
1 tablespoon dark sesame oil or more to taste
1 tablespoon peanut or vegetable oil

• Preheat oven to 300°. Heat 2 quarts water in large deep skillet to boiling.

• Cook noodles in boiling water 1 minute; drain in colander. While noodles are still warm, drizzle with soy sauce and sesame oil. Toss to coat; set aside.

• Heat peanut oil in large nonstick skillet over medium-high heat until smoking. Add noodles; press over the bottom to make a thick pancake. Cook, without burning, until light brown and crisp, 3 minutes. Turn pancake over. Cook, adding up to 1/4 cup water if necessary to prevent burning, until crisp, about 3 minutes more. Keep warm in oven on baking sheet or in skillet if oven-safe. Serve pancake on a heated round platter.

Crunchy Fruit Bouchées

4 ripe finger bananas, peeled, cut crosswise into
  1-inch chunks, or 2 cups peach chunks, seedless
  grapes, or pitted cherries
1 (7-ounce) container chocolate ice-cream
  shell coating

• Freeze fruit on parchment-lined baking sheet in freezer until ice-cold, about 15 minutes.

• Heat chocolate coating as package label directs and pour over the fruit. Serve immediately or refrigerate until ready to serve.

A Good Luck Chinese Dinner

• Steamed Fish with Sweet Chili Sauce • Vegetable Lo Mein Stir-Fry • Caramelized Pineapple

MAKES 4 SERVINGS

In many Asian cultures a whole fish symbolizes totality, and eating a fish head is thought to bring much luck. But that's not for everyone; you're not wimping out if you use fillets. You'll find the Chinese sweet chili sauce a versatile condiment, and it's good as a salad dressing without any additions.

GAME PLAN

1. Heat water for noodles. Preheat broiler. Mix steaming sauce.
2. Steam whole fish (wait about 8 minutes to steam fillets). Broil pineapple.
3. Cook and drain noodles; stir-fry with vegetables.

Steamed Fish with Sweet Chili Sauce

1 (2-pound) cleaned whole fish on the bone (with
   head on) such as sea bass or red snapper or 4
   (6-to 8-ounce) fillets
1 teaspoon salt

STEAMING SAUCE

1 green onion, trimmed, cut into 2-inch slivers
1 tablespoon grated peeled fresh ginger
3 tablespoons Chinese sweet chili sauce
1 tablespoon Chinese black vinegar or cider vinegar

• Prepare wok or wide steamer with boiling water. Rinse fish under gently running cold water and pat dry with paper towels. If using whole fish, make 2 or 3 diagonal slashes to the bone on both sides. Sprinkle fish inside and out with salt. Place fish in a deep bowl and place bowl in wok or steamer over boiling water.

• Combine sauce ingredients and mix well. Pour over fish. Cover and steam until cooked through, allowing 10 minutes for each inch thickness of fish, 12 to 15 minutes. (Cook fillets 4 to 6 minutes, depending on thickness.) Carefully remove lid and serve immediately.

Vegetable Lo Mein Stir-Fry

2 (3-ounce) packages ramen noodles (discard
    seasoning packets)
2 teaspoons vegetable oil
4 teaspoons grated peeled fresh gingerroot
1/4 teaspoon crushed red-pepper flakes
1 red bell pepper, seeded, thinly sliced
1 yellow bell pepper, seeded, thinly sliced
1 bunch green onions, trimmed, quartered
    lengthwise, cut crosswise into 2-inch slivers
2 tablespoons roasted garlic teriyaki sauce or
    other favorite stir-fry sauce

• Heat 1 quart water in large saucepan to boiling.
Add noodles and cook 3 minutes. Drain and set aside.

• Heat oil in large nonstick skillet or wok over
medium-high heat; add ginger and pepper flakes; stir-
fry 30 seconds. Add bell peppers and onions; stir-fry
until crisp-tender, 3 minutes. Add sauce and noodles;
stir-fry until heated through, about 2 minutes.

Caramelized Pineapple

4 (3/4-inch-thick) canned or fresh pineapple rings
2 tablespoons maple syrup or honey
2 tablespoons rum
1/4 teaspoon freshly ground pepper

• Preheat broiler. Line broiler pan with foil; arrange
pineapple in pan. Mix syrup, rum, and pepper; brush
half of mixture over pineapple. Broil 4 inches from
heat until glaze is caramelized, about 4 minutes. Turn
pineapple and brush with remaining glaze. Broil until
caramelized.

Peking Duck Without Fuss

• Streamlined Pan-Fried Peking Duck • Hoisin Duck Sauce • In-an-Instant Strawberry Ice Cream

MAKES 4 SERVINGS

This elaborate, "we're not worthy," seemingly restaurant-only dish is really so easy to make at home. Using just the breasts cuts out some of the delightful skin from a whole duck, but it also cuts down the preparation time.

GAME PLAN
1. Score and cook duck. Make sauce.
2. Make ice cream; freeze.
3. Steam pancakes; slice duck.

Streamlined Pan-Fried Peking Duck

2 boneless duck-breast halves (2 pounds), excess
    fat removed, patted dry
2 tablespoons honey, sugar, or molasses
2 tablespoons dry sherry
kosher salt and freshly ground black pepper to taste
2 bunches green onions, trimmed, shredded
12 to 16 mandarin pancakes (from a Chinese
    restaurant) or store-bought crêpes or 2 (14-inch)
    sandwich wraps
Hoisin Duck Sauce (recipe follows)

• Score skin side of breasts 1/4-inch deep in a 1/2-inch crisscross pattern. Mix honey and sherry; rub over duck. Sprinkle liberally with salt and pepper and rub in.

• Heat a heavy large skillet over medium heat. Place breasts skin side down in pan. Cook, basting meat with hot fat to cook from top and adjusting heat so skin doesn't burn, until fat is rendered and skin is browned, 10 minutes. Turn breasts over and cook 4 minutes longer for medium-rare. Remove to cutting board; cover and let rest at least 5 minutes.

• Place onions in shallow dish. Steam pancakes in microwave or steamer and keep warm in a moist tea towel.

• To serve: Thinly slice duck breasts lengthwise and then in strips. Each guest should brush duck sauce onto one side of a pancake, top with a big pinch of onions, then a slice of duck. Fold one side of pancake over long side of duck; fold up one short end. Fold over other long side. Eat with open end going into mouth first. (For large wraps: Spread with sauce, sprinkle with onion and arrange strips of duck on top. Roll up; cut each roll crosswise into 4 pieces.)

Hoisin Duck Sauce

1/2 cup hoisin sauce
2 tablespoons water
2 teaspoons dark sesame oil

• Mix hoisin, water, and oil in a shallow dish.

Makes about 1/2 cup.

In-an-Instant Strawberry Ice Cream

You can use any frozen fruit, even if it doesn't come packaged. About 4 heaping cups will equal 1 pound.

1 cup cold heavy cream
1/3 cup superfine or regular granulated sugar
1 (1-pound) bag frozen strawberries

• Combine cold cream and sugar in a food processor and process until mixture has thickened, a few seconds, stopping to scrape down sides with a spatula.

• Add a few berries and process using pulse motion. Repeat until all berries are used and mixture is smooth. Serve immediately or transfer to a freezer-safe plastic storage container and freeze up to 3 hours. Let soften slightly at room temperature before serving.

Makes 4 to 6 servings.

At-Home Celebration Dinner

• Hot Cheesy Crabmeat Dip • Any Steak in a Port • Creamed Pearl Onions • *Fresh Fruit Salad*

MAKES 4 SERVINGS

Crab and steak are ingredients usually reserved for special occasions, and when the time comes, this is a perfect "surf and turf" menu.

GAME PLAN

1. Make the crab dip; keep warm.
2. Make the onions; keep warm.
3. Fry the steaks; make sauce.

Hot Cheesy Crabmeat Dip

1/2 cup (1 stick) unsalted butter

1 bunch green onions, trimmed, chopped, with some green part included

2 cups heavy cream

4 ounces cheddar cheese spread with tomatoes and basil or shredded jalapeño-jack cheese

1 pound jumbo lump crabmeat, gently picked over for bits of shells

Tabasco sauce to taste

celery stalks for dipping

• Melt butter in a heavy saucepan over medium-high heat. Add onions; sauté until soft, 3 minutes. Add cream and whisk until smooth. Stir in cheese spread and blend until smooth. Gently fold in crabmeat and season with Tabasco.

• Scrape into a chafing dish or fondue pot and keep warm. Serve with celery for dipping.

Any Steak in a Port

You can grill or broil the steaks or cook them on the stovetop in a grill pan and make the sauce separately. Start by sautéing the shallots in 1 tablespoon butter to make up for the pan drippings.

4 (6- to 8-ounce) boneless steaks (sirloin, rib-eye, tenderloin), 1/2-inch-thick, at room temperature
1 tablespoon oil
kosher salt and freshly ground pepper to taste
1 large shallot, chopped
1 teaspoon chopped fresh rosemary
1/2 cup port wine
4 tablespoons unsalted butter, softened, in bits
crushed pink peppercorns to taste

• Rub steaks on both sides with oil, then salt and pepper. Heat a large heavy nonstick or cast-iron skillet over medium-high heat until smoking. Cook steaks 2 to 3 minutes on both sides (for medium-rare). Remove with tongs to warm plate. Cover and keep warm.

• Add shallot and rosemary to drippings in pan and sauté 1 minute. Add wine; stir, scraping up browned bits. Boil until reduced by half. Add 3 tablespoons butter and whisk until melted and sauce is thickened. Pour over steaks. Dot with remaining butter; sprinkle with peppercorns.

Creamed Pearl Onions

2 tablespoons unsalted butter
1 (10-ounce) package frozen pearl onions, thawed
1 tablespoon all-purpose flour
1 cup half-and-half or heavy cream
2 tablespoons dry white vermouth
1 teaspoon herbes de Provence

• Melt butter in 2-quart saucepan over medium-high heat and stir in onions. Sauté over medium heat until hot. Sprinkle with flour and stir until blended. Gradually add half-and-half, stirring until smooth. Stir in vermouth and herbs. Heat to boiling, stirring. Cook, stirring, until thickened, about 4 minutes.

Beef Lover's Classic Stroganoff

• Beef Tenderloin Stroganoff • Confetti Noodles • Steamed Baby Carrots

MAKES 4 SERVINGS

Named after the 19th-century Russian diplomat Count Paul Stroganov, this dish has gone so mainstream that it's an American comfort food. Serve it with egg noodles and you'll probably start to miss your mom.

GAME PLAN

1. Heat water for noodles. Sauté onions.
2. Cook carrots; keep warm. Cook noodles; mix "confetti."
3. Brown beef; finish stroganoff. Toss noodles with confetti.

Beef Tenderloin Stroganoff

Why two skillets? Otherwise you'd have to brown the meat in 2 batches and that would take twice as long.

3 tablespoons roasted-garlic teriyaki sauce

1 tablespoon powdered mustard

1 teaspoon sweet Hungarian paprika

4 tablespoons unsalted butter

4 tablespoons vegetable oil

2 red onions, quartered, finely sliced

1 pound mushrooms, thinly sliced

1½ to 2 pounds fillet of beef, trimmed, thinly sliced, cut into ¼-inch strips

1 pint sour cream

salt and freshly ground pepper to taste

• Blend teriyaki sauce, mustard, and paprika. Set aside.

• Melt 1 tablespoon butter in 1 tablespoon oil in each of 2 large nonstick skillets over medium-high heat. Add half the onions to each pan; sauté until caramelized, 10 minutes. Add half the mushrooms to each pan; sauté until softened, about 3 minutes. Scrape onion mixture into a bowl.

• Melt 1 tablespoon butter in 1 tablespoon oil in each of the skillets over medium-high heat. Add half the beef to each skillet; sauté until lightly browned, 2 minutes. Stir half the sour cream, mustard mixture, and onion mixture into each skillet; heat to simmering. Season to taste with salt and pepper.

Confetti Noodles

salt
8 ounces wide egg noodles or fresh fettuccine
1 (7-ounce) jar chopped pimientos, drained
1/4 cup snipped fresh chives
1/4 cup sliced black olives
1 teaspoon golden mustard seeds
freshly ground black pepper to taste

• Heat 3 quarts salted water to boiling in a large, deep skillet. Add noodles and cook as package label directs. While noodles cook, combine remaining ingredients in large serving bowl and mix.

• Drain noodles, reserving 1/4 cup cooking liquid. Add noodles to pimiento mixture; toss to coat, adding enough reserved cooking liquid to make noodles moist.

Steamed Baby Carrots

1 (1-pound) bag peeled baby carrots
1/4 cup water
salt and freshly ground pepper to taste
2 tablespoons unsalted butter, softened
1 tablespoon chopped or torn fresh parsley or
*   mint leaves*

• Combine carrots, water, salt, and pepper in microwave-safe bowl. Cover with microwave-safe plastic wrap; cook on high power until tender, 5 to 8 minutes. Add butter and parsley; toss.

Fruity Breakfast for Dinner

• Tropical Smoothies • Huevos Rancheros • Ginger-Juiced Fruit Salad • Homemade Muesli

MAKES 4 SERVINGS

Relax over the Sunday papers in the evening. A flavorful breakfast for dinner gets everyone hungry and makes the most of time with friends.

GAME PLAN
1. Preheat oven. Make and bake muesli.
2. Make fruit salad and smoothies.
3. Heat tortillas and prepare eggs.

Tropical Smoothies

1 (12-ounce) can papaya or mango nectar

1 pint frozen lemon or vanilla yogurt, in chunks

2 cups peeled, seeded papaya or mango, in chunks

1/2 teaspoon vanilla extract

mint sprigs for garnish

• Combine nectar, yogurt, papaya, and vanilla in blender; blend on high speed until smooth. Pour into glasses; garnish with mint sprigs.

Huevos Rancheros

4 flour tortillas
2 tablespoons unsalted butter
4 eggs
1/4 cup shredded extra-sharp Cheddar cheese
1/4 cup shredded Monterey Jack cheese (with or without jalapeños)
1/2 cup bottled salsa
1/2 to 1 cup guacamole or 1 avocado, peeled, pitted, sliced

• Heat tortillas one at a time in large nonstick skillet over medium heat on both sides. Wrap in foil and keep warm.

• Melt butter in skillet; fry eggs to desired doneness, 3 minutes or until set. Sprinkle with cheeses.

• Place tortillas on plates; top with eggs. Serve with salsa and guacamole.

Ginger-Juiced Fruit Salad

2 cups papaya chunks
1 pint blueberries, washed, drained
1/2 pint raspberries, washed, drained
1/2 cup each green, red, and purple seedless grapes
1/2 cup ginger syrup (store-bought or see recipe page 217)
mint sprigs for garnish

• Combine fruits and syrup in large bowl; toss to mix. Garnish with mint.

Homemade Muesli

Serve with milk or yogurt.

nonstick cooking spray
1/2 cup honey
4 tablespoons unsalted butter
3 cups rolled oats
1 cup shaved coconut pieces
3/4 cup flaked unblanched almonds
3/4 cup wheat germ
1/2 cup chopped pitted dates
1/2 cup chopped dried papaya
1/3 cup dried cranberries, blueberries, or strawberries

• Preheat oven to 425°. Line large baking sheet with foil; grease with cooking spray.

• Heat honey and butter in small saucepan over medium heat, stirring to blend, until butter melts. In large bowl, mix remaining ingredients. Pour honey butter over mixture and stir to coat.

• Spread muesli out on baking sheet; bake (even if oven is not up to temperature), stirring after 5 minutes, 10 minutes. Use immediately or, to crisp mixture for longer storage, turn off oven and let mixture bake until oven is cold. Store in airtight container.

Makes about 6 servings.

Homemade Versions of Store-Bought Products

Sun-Dried Tomato Pesto

Stir a dollop of this concentrated sauce into soup, add it to a pasta cream sauce, or whisk it into mayonnaise, sour cream, crème fraîche, or softened cream cheese for an instant dip or spread. That's just the beginning. It's the perfect single slather on crostini after the bread is toasted, and on fish, poultry, meat, and tofu before grilling.

2 large cloves garlic, crushed through a press
3 tablespoons olive oil
2 tablespoons tomato paste
1 (28-ounce) can plum tomatoes, preferably
  San Marzano
1/2 teaspoon freshly ground pepper, or more to taste
pinch of cayenne pepper, or more to taste
1 cup marinated sun-dried tomatoes with their oil

- Heat garlic in oil in large skillet over medium heat until softened and fragrant but not browned, about 3 minutes. Add tomato paste; sauté until it starts to stick to the pan and turns a rust color. Add tomatoes and their juices, ground pepper, and cayenne; stir, scraping up browned bits. Mash tomatoes with a potato masher until evenly chunky. Simmer over medium-low heat, partially covered, until very thick but still with some juices, 20 to 30 minutes.

- Drain sun-dried tomatoes, reserving the oil; place sun-dried tomatoes in food processor with a ladle full of tomato sauce. Pulse to mix and then purée. Add remaining tomato sauce. With machine running, pour in oil from sun-dried tomatoes through the feed tube.

- Pour into a bowl; taste and adjust seasonings. Cool; remove what you need to jar and refrigerate until needed (keeps 3 to 4 days). Spoon remainder into 1/2-cup freezer containers and freeze.

Makes about 2 1/2 cups.

Pesto

2 garlic cloves
2 tablespoons pine nuts
1 cup packed fresh basil leaves
3 tablespoons freshly grated Parmigiano-Reggiano
  cheese
3 tablespoons freshly grated Pecorino Romano cheese
1/4 cup extra-virgin olive oil

- Place garlic in food processor; mince. Add nuts and basil; pulse and process until finely chopped. Add cheeses; with machine running, pour in oil through feed tube. Process until just incorporated; you want to have an interesting texture, not a perfectly smooth purée.

Makes about 1 cup.

Sambal Oelek

1 cup whole fresh hot red chilies
2 garlic cloves, quartered lengthwise
1 small onion, quartered lengthwise
2 tablespoons sugar
2 tablespoons fresh lemon juice or lime juice
1 teaspoon salt
1/4 cup water

• Trim stem ends off chiles. Place them in food processor; pulse until split and cut up into rough 1-inch pieces, stirring without touching pepper with your hands, to loosen from blades if necessary. Add garlic, onion, sugar, juice, and salt; pulse until mixed. With machine running, pour in water through feed tube. Process until mixture is a paste.

• Transfer mixture to a small skillet or saucepan; simmer partially covered over medium heat 10 minutes.

Makes about 1 cup.

Harissa

Use as a seasoning or for a spicy sauce for couscous, thinning it with an equal amount of water and a little olive oil and lemon juice.

1/2 cup mixed stemmed and seeded dried ancho,
*   New Mexican, and guajillo chilies*
1 tablespoon chopped roasted red pepper
1 small garlic clove, crushed through a press
1/4 teaspoon ground coriander
1/4 teaspoon ground Middle Eastern cumin or
*   caraway seeds*
1/4 teaspoon salt or more to taste
olive oil for storing

• Place dried chilies in a small bowl; pour boiling water on top to cover chilies. Cover; let stand 30 minutes to 1 hour. Drain though a sieve, pressing out extra moisture. Place in a mortar and pound to a paste. Add roasted red pepper, garlic, coriander, and cumin; pound to blend into chilies. Season with salt; scrape into a jar. Pour a layer of oil on top; seal and store in refrigerator.

Makes about 1/4 cup.

Salsa Fresca

Everyone has his own recipe for salsa; this one is designed to be adapted to the family palate. Be sure to wear disposable gloves when handling chilies or use a fork to pin them down to the cutting board as you slice them and remove the seeds.

1¹/2 pounds tomatoes, seeded, coarsely chopped
1 small onion, finely chopped
2 jalapeños or 1 to 2 serrano (hotter) chilies,
  seeded, finely chopped
2 tablespoons chopped fresh cilantro
2 tablespoons fresh lime juice
salt to taste

● Pulse tomatoes in food processor until finely chopped. Pour into a bowl; stir in remaining ingredients. Keeps 2 to 3 days in the refrigerator.

Makes about 3 cups.

In-a-Pinch Asian Fish Sauce

4 anchovy fillets
1/4 cup plus 2 teaspoons low-sodium soy sauce
4 teaspoons water

● Mash anchovies to a paste in a bowl with a fork. Stir in soy sauce and water.

Makes about ¹/3 cup.

Tapenade

Tapéno means caper in the local dialect of Provence.

1 cup pitted Niçoise or other imported black olives
2 tablespoons salted capers, rinsed
2 tablespoons extra-virgin olive oil
1 garlic clove, crushed through a press
4 to 8 anchovy fillets, to taste
freshly ground pepper to taste
fresh lemon juice to taste (optional)

● Combine ingredients in a mortar and crush to a coarse paste.

Makes about 1 cup.

Balsamic Vinaigrette

1 tablespoon minced shallots (optional)
1/2 teaspoon minced garlic
1/4 cup balsamic vinegar
1/4 cup extra-virgin olive oil
salt and freshly ground pepper to taste

● Mix shallot, garlic, and vinegar together in a small bowl. Gradually add oil, whisking until mixture thickens. Season with salt and pepper.

Makes about ¹/2 cup.

Red-Wine Vinaigrette

2 tablespoons red-wine vinegar
1 tablespoon minced shallot (optional)
1 tablespoon Dijon mustard
1/2 cup extra-virgin olive oil
salt and freshly ground pepper to taste

• Mix vinegar, shallot, and mustard in a small bowl. Gradually add oil, whisking until mixture thickens. Season with salt and pepper.

Makes about 1/2 cup.

Raspberry Vinaigrette

The mint leaves are best in a dressing that is going to be used up all at once.

2 tablespoons raspberry vinegar
2 tablespoons rice vinegar
1 to 11/2 teaspoons sugar
1/3 cup light olive oil or vegetable oil
1/4 cup loosely packed fresh mint leaves, chopped
*   (optional)*
salt and freshly ground pepper to taste

• Mix vinegars and 1 teaspoon sugar in a small bowl. Gradually add oil, whisking until mixture thickens. Whisk in mint. Season with salt and pepper. Taste; blend in additional 1/2 teaspoon sugar if needed.

Makes about 1/2 cup.

Citrus Vinaigrette

3 tablespoons fresh orange juice
2 tablespoons fresh lemon juice
1 to 11/2 teaspoons sugar
11/2 teaspoons Dijon mustard
1/3 cup light olive oil or vegetable oil
salt and freshly ground pepper to taste

• Mix juices, 1 teaspoon sugar, and the mustard in a small bowl. Gradually add oil, whisking until mixture thickens. Season with salt and pepper. Taste; whisk in additional 1/2 teaspoon sugar if needed.

Makes about 2/3 cup.

Herb Vinaigrette

2 garlic cloves, crushed through a press
1/3 cup red-wine vinegar
11/2 tablespoons dried Italian herb seasoning
11/2 tablespoons Dijon mustard
1/4 cup vegetable oil
1 cup extra virgin olive oil
salt and freshly ground pepper to taste

• Mix garlic, vinegar, herbs, and mustard in a small bowl, blender, or food processor. Whisk or pour in the oils slowly, blending until mixture thickens. Season with salt and pepper.

Makes about 2 cups.

Caesar Salad Dressing

1 egg yolk
2 tablespoons balsamic vinegar
2 tablespoons fresh lemon juice
3 to 5 anchovy fillets
2 garlic cloves, crushed through a press
1 tablespoon grainy Dijon mustard
1 teaspoon dried thyme leaves
1 teaspoon finely grated lemon zest
1/2 cup vegetable oil
2/3 to 1 cup olive oil
salt and freshly ground pepper to taste

• Combine egg yolk, vinegar, lemon juice, anchovies, garlic, mustard, thyme, and zest in food processor; process until smooth. With machine running, pour in vegetable oil in a thin stream. Scrape down sides of bowl. With machine running, pour in 2/3 cup olive oil in a thin stream. Taste and season with salt and pepper; add as much remaining olive oil as desired to make a creamy, pourable dressing.

Makes about 13/4 cups.

Vanilla Syrup

21/2 cups water
11/4 cups sugar
1/2 vanilla bean, split, or 1 tablespoon vanilla
*   extract*

• Combine the water, sugar, and vanilla bean (but not the extract) in a large saucepan and heat to boiling over medium-high heat, stirring until the sugar dissolves. Reduce heat to prevent boiling if sugar has not dissolved all the way, and then once it has, increase the heat so the syrup boils. Boil 1 minute.

• Let the syrup cool. Remove the vanilla bean or stir in the vanilla extract. Store in refrigerator for up to 1 month.

Makes about 3 cups.

Ginger Syrup

11/4 cups water
1 cup sugar
8 ounces peeled fresh gingerroot, minced in food
*   processor*

• Combine the water and sugar in a large saucepan and heat to boiling over medium-high heat, stirring until the sugar dissolves. Add ginger; heat to boiling. Reduce heat and simmer 5 minutes. Let stand until cool; strain. Store in refrigerator.

Makes about 11/4 cups.

Quick Preserved Lemons

You can find preserved lemons in Indian and Middle Eastern grocery stores, and there are recipes for the long process required to ripen fresh lemons. This recipe is a quicker, 5-day process.

3 lemons
2 tablespoons salt
2 cups water

● Make 8 fine, 2-inch vertical incisions around the peel of each lemon, not cutting deep enough to reach the pith. Stir salt in water in medium saucepan until dissolved; add prepared lemons. Cover; heat to boiling over medium heat. Reduce heat and simmer until peels are very soft, about 20 minutes. Let stand until cool.

● Place lemons in a clean jar, cover with cooking brine, and leave at room temperature for 5 days. Remove lemons as needed. Rinse before using. Discard pulp if desired, but both peel and pulp can be used. Store in refrigerator for up to 1 month.

Makes 3 preserved lemons.

Easy Lemon Curd

2 egg yolks
1 (14-ounce) can sweetened condensed milk
1 teaspoon freshly grated lemon zest
1/4 cup fresh lemon juice

● Combine egg yolks, sweetened condensed milk, lemon zest, and lemon juice in a medium bowl and whisk until blended. Cover with plastic wrap and refrigerate until set, about 1 hour.

Makes about 2 cups.

Peach Sauce

*1 (8-ounce) can sliced peaches or 1 cup fresh or
    thawed frozen peaches*
orange juice (if using fresh or frozen peaches)

● Drain peaches, reserving liquid. Purée peaches in food processor, adding enough reserved liquid or orange juice to make a coating consistency.

Makes 4 servings.

Index